ENDO

Two things draw me to this book. First, the writer himself. Bill Wellons embodies the values and principles he expresses. He is a true inside-out leader who has greatly enriched my life over the past 40 years. Secondly, this book is a goldmine of insights. It identifies and articulates the basic building blocks of authentic leadership. We know all too well gifted leaders who fail us and God's kingdom because their interior life has been left hollow or uncultivated. They ignore the warning that *"God is not like man and looks not on outward appearances but on the heart"*, 1 Samuel 16:7. If you're a leader, give your heart a life-altering gift and drink deeply at the well of *What Really Matters!*

— **DR. ROBERT LEWIS,**
Pastor, Founder-Men's Fraternity.

When it comes to developing high capacity ministry leaders, Bill is the guy. He's done it, is doing it, and now gets to come alongside you through this book. His 40+ years of experience being in the trenches and coaching people through it are dripping off of these pages, so don't miss this book.

— **DANIEL IM,**
author of *No Silver Bullets*,
coauthor of *Planting Missional Churches*,
director of church multiplication at NewChurches.com,
teaching pastor, and podcaster.

God gives us many kinds of gifts. When he brings people into our lives who help conform us into the image of his Son it is truly a tremendous gift. That is exactly how I feel about Bill Wellons and the impact he has made on me and my husband, Dave over the past decade we've known his family. What a Christian leader needs more than any trick-of-the-trade is to experience the life of God in the soul of the leader. I'm so excited Bill has written down the wisdom he has gained from his experiences of following God through the path of leadership.

— GLORIA FURMAN,
author of *Missional Motherhood*,
Alive in Him, and *The Pastor's Wife*.

Leadership is dangerous. A quick look at the number of leaders who have fallen across our leadership landscape is sobering. That's why I'm so thankful for Bill Wellons and his leader saving book, *What Really Matters! The Seven Values of an Inside-Out Leader*. Wellons' takes leaders in a fresh, yet ancient, direction that enables leaders to go further faster without falling. Combining biblical truth with the wisdom that can only be learned through several decades of leading and training leaders, *What Really Matters!* is a steady, inspiring guide that belongs in every leader's hands. Once you read it, like me, you'll realize it's one of those books that belongs on the annual reading shelf. I highly recommend it!

— DR. JEDIDIAH COPPENGER,
Lead Pastor of Redemption City Church in Franklin, TN.

Bill is a gift to the body that has gone as a secret weapon. He has been a blessing to tons of young leaders all over the world. The principles in this book were honed in his own life and passed on to several generations of leaders. I pray this book blesses you as it has blessed our lives on every level of leadership.

— **DR. ERIC MASON,**
Lead Pastor of Epiphany Fellowship, Philadelphia, PA
and author of several books including *Woke Church,*
Unleashed, Manhood Restored, and *Beat God to the Punch.*

"I have watched Bill Wellons living out the seven principles in *What Really Matters* in his own leadership. If leadership is influence, perhaps the greatest leaders influence our heart and mind without the need of a position or title. This is what Bill has learned and distilled down for us. I find his thoughtful questions to be more helpful than a boat load of 'smart answers.'

— **LLOYD REEB,**
author *From Success to Significance*
and Spokesperson, the Halftime Institute.

My mentor, Bill Wellons, has been living this book long before he wrote it. These seven chapters carry the potential to deeply grow you as a leader. I'd be a much less healthy leader without the presence and care of Bill Wellons who has been coaching me in these seven values for many years.

— **JUSTIN BUZZARD,**
Lead Pastor of Garden City Church in Silicon Valley
and author of *The Big Story,*
Date Your Wife, and *Why Cities Matter.*

I had the privilege of learning some of these principles firsthand from Bill as a personal friend and longtime mentor. I am grateful that he has taken time to write out these truths so that you can learn from his wisdom and grow as a leader. This book has a reflective style with an emphasis on identity. Taken to heart, these seven values have the potential to change your life.

— **DHATI LEWIS,**
Lead Pastor of Blueprint Church,
Executive Director of Community Restoration,
NAMB and author of *Among Wolves.*

I consider Bill Wellons one of the most important mentors in my leadership journey. I know I'm one of many that think of him this way. The quiet, behind the scenes impact he's had on church planting and church leadership around the world is amazing. Being mentored by Bill is a real gift of grace, both for the leader and for Jesus's Church. That's why I'm so glad he wrote this book. It's almost as good as getting to sit across the table from him and learn what it means to be a leader, as he shares from his Godly wisdom and nearly fifty years of ministry experience.

— **ELLIOT GRUDEM,**
Founder and President, Leaders Collective.

King Solomon was said to have been given wisdom and understanding beyond measure. And I can't prove it, but Bill Wellons has to be a descendant of the King. *What Really Matters* is loaded with wisdom and should be required reading for every leader, manager, husband and wife, and importantly, EVERY parent. This transformational book will not only make you a better person, but those that you are developing and discipling as well. I'm buying a copy for every one of our adult children--they'll be better equipped personally and more effective as they parent their children!

— **DR. DENNIS RAINEY,**
Host of FamilyLife Today
and Co-Founder of FamilyLife.

"I have had the joy and privilege of knowing Bill Wellons for more than thirty years. He is a portrait of what he writes about in What Really Matters! Several years ago Bill shared with our staff team what he has now shaped into this wonderful book. What he shared that day struck a chord in our hearts. Although there are countless books on leadership, this book is different. It points to the soul of a leader and the relationship between the leader's heart and how he or she thinks and acts. It is a call to authenticity, integrity and integration. I love this book!"

— **DR. CRAWFORD W. LORITTS**
Author, Speaker, Radio Host
Sr. Pastor Fellowship Bible Church
Roswell, Georgia

WHAT REALLY MATTERS!

The Seven Values of an Inside-Out Leader

Lisa of us, more of Him — a winning combination every time!

Bill Wellons

Bill Wellons

What Really Matters! The Seven Values of an Inside-Out Leader

Editing services by ChristianEditingServices.com.

ISBN: 978-1-7325185-0-6

What Really Matters! is dedicated to
Christian leaders, young and old.

WHAT REALLY MATTERS!
The Seven Values of an Inside-Out Leader

ACKNOWLEDGMENTS

The fourth chapter of *What Really Matters!* addresses the incredible value of team. I benefitted immensely while writing this book with the assistance of a very gifted team of people. Carolyn, my wife of forty-seven years; Dotty Hendren; Susan Petty; and Ann Blair provided wonderful insights while editing the manuscript. David Petty, newspaper veteran and close friend, generously gave his time and talent to this project. He supported me, challenged me, and mentored me as a writer.

Published authors Robert Lewis, (my ministry partner for over thirty years), Gloria Furman, Jed Coppenger; along with Rebecca Price, a former publishing executive; and Tad Krug, an avid reader, offered constructive criticism and creative ideas about the content of the book.

The backing and encouragement from these team members made me feel loved. I deeply appreciate and value all of you. You remind me of the wisdom of

Solomon: "Two are better than one, because they have a good reward for their toil. For if they fall, one will lift up his fellow" (Ecclesiastes 4:9–10).

PREFACE

Christian leaders are under enormous pressure to perform. Image is more valued than substance, reputation is prized over character, and climbing the ladder of success is king. Sadly, the world we live in not only reinforces these values but also rewards them.

Literally thousands of books have been written on leadership. This being the case, it may seem foolhardy to offer yet another one. I am alarmed, however, about the performance-based culture in which we find ourselves. Furthermore, I am convinced that God has moved me to share with you what He has taught me about what really matters in a leader's life.

This book is not an autobiography or a self-help guide to becoming a better leader. It is a book about understanding the character of one's soul. Rather than offering a series of steps to becoming a successful leader, this book presents a transforming process of *being* rather than just *doing*—an integration of one's head with one's heart. It is designed to take readers on a journey toward wholeness where they long to serve and glorify the One greater than themselves.

The following pages address seven heart-level leadership values that are essential to a leader's emotional and spiritual maturity. I firmly believe that the way leaders receive and incarnate these values will determine the impact of their leadership on others and the legacy of their lives.

The most profound learning laboratory of my life was leading the elder board of Fellowship Bible Church in Little Rock, Arkansas, for more than thirty years. This experience taught me about leadership, decision-making, myself, and trusting God.

From 1977 to 2007 the Lord grew our church from a group of thirty founders to nearly six thousand people. We never envisioned such growth. During this time we witnessed God accomplish some extraordinary things— transforming lives, providing financially, saving marriages, raising up leaders, granting our church favor in the community, and so much more.

Our leadership team encountered a multitude of challenges. Our learning curve was a steep one, but somehow God guided us through our failures and our successes. We were not perfect leaders. He was!

Church planting was a part of Fellowship from the beginning. During the first twenty years of the church, God used us to establish fifteen new churches. Twice we intentionally split our church to launch churches in nearby communities.

In 1999 we started a separate non-profit organization, Fellowship Associates, to develop a leadership program for church planters. Upon completing my role as founder, teaching pastor, and chairman of the elder board, I transitioned to direct this leadership residency program.

Fellowship Associates is both a finishing school and a leadership incubator. It allows men who know they have been called by God to lead a new church to take their first steps toward doing so while being coached and encouraged at every point in their journey.

To date, the Lord has granted us the privilege of establishing one hundred gospel-centered, community-influencing, church-planting churches. In addition, more than one hundred churches have been started by those churches. Furthermore, we have launched eight other leadership residencies.

Several years ago God impressed upon me the need to look back vocationally and record the leadership lessons He had taught me. After working on this for several months, I noticed that in each lesson there was an emphasis on personal change, developing stronger character virtues *instead of leadership tips!*

As I have shared what I have learned in formal presentations, the response has always been encouraging. Often someone asks, "Have you ever thought of putting these ideas in a book?" Thus my firm belief is God wants me to share what He has taught me with a larger audience. That audience is Christian leaders, both young and old.

To get the most out of this book, I urge you to read it slowly, similar to reflecting over a devotional.

Following the conclusion of each chapter is a section called "Another Leader's Journey." These personal stories were written by leaders whom I have trained. They communicate each man's unique perspectives and experiences about the subject matter just read.

Next is "Reflect and Record," an application opportunity inviting you to answer some questions and spend some time writing down what you believe God is saying to your heart.

The final page, entitled "Remember," highlights three foundational truths summarizing each chapter.

Chapter 1

SELF-AWARENESS

*"The foundation of our identity resides in our
life-giving relationship with the Source of Life.
Any identity that exists apart from this
relationship is an illusion."*
– David Benner

D O YOU REALLY KNOW YOURSELF? Self-
awareness is an essential leadership trait, but
chances are good that you have several blind spots. In
fact, according to well-known psychologist Dr. Tasha
Eurich, "95 percent of people think they're self-aware,
but the real number is closer to 10–15 percent." Eurich,
who for the last fifteen years has coached Fortune 500

executives, adds, "I always joke that on a good day, 80% of us are lying to ourselves about whether we're lying to ourselves."[1]

John the Baptist was strange in appearance—Matthew described him as wearing "a garment of camel's hair and a leather belt around his waist; and his food was locusts and wild honey" (Matthew 3:4 NASB)— but he was a self-aware leader who was confident about the God-given purpose for his life. His message was brief, bold, and blunt: "Repent, for the Kingdom of Heaven is at hand" (Matthew 3:2 NASB).

He was crystal clear about who he was and who he was not. According to Isaiah's prophecy, John was the forerunner to prepare the way for someone else and then get out of the way. That is exactly what John did. When questioned about his ministry, he replied, "'I am not the Christ,' but, 'I have been sent ahead of Him.' . . . He must increase, but I must decrease" (John 3:28, 30 NASB).

These are the powerful words of a self-aware, emotionally secure leader. Such self-awareness is a leader's single greatest need—integrating one's head and heart.

After surveying nearly two hundred global companies, Daniel Goleman presented his findings in an article in the *Harvard Business Review* entitled "What Makes a Great Leader." He concluded that emotional intelligence, or self-awareness, "is the essential element of leadership. Without it, a person can have the best training in the world, an incisive, analytical mind, and an endless supply of smart ideas, but still won't make a great leader."[2]

What then are the hallmarks of self-aware leaders?

- Self-aware leaders understand that their exterior life flows out of their interior life. Healthy leadership always proceeds from being to doing, from inside to outside.

- Self-aware leaders know the strengths and weaknesses of their personality. They understand their passions and what energizes them as a leader. They know what they do well and what they do not do well. Actually, the latter of these two is the most difficult to admit.

- Self-aware leaders comprehend what God has designed them to contribute to others as well as what they need from others. This balance of giving and receiving is critical when putting together a good team. In other words, great hiring starts with knowing oneself!

- Self-aware leaders are in touch with their inner motivations and emotions. They understand how these affect them as well as those they lead.

The apostle Paul described a battle raging within the heart of every person. It is a conflict between flesh and spirit, darkness and light, immaturity and maturity. Notice the contrasting results of each in the following passage:

But I say, walk by the Spirit, and you will not gratify the desires of the flesh. . . . Now the works of the flesh are evident: sexual immorality, impurity, sensuality, idolatry, sorcery, enmity, strife, jealousy, fits of anger, rivalries, dissensions, divisions, envy, drunkenness, orgies, and things like these. . . . But the fruit of the Spirit is love, joy, peace, patience, kindness, goodness, faithfulness, gentleness, self-control. (Galatians 5:16, 19–21, 22–23)

These two opposing natures are often called the *false self* and the *true self*. Simply put, the false self seeks its identity apart from a relationship with Jesus Christ, whereas the true self seeks its identity only in Jesus Christ.

Brennan Manning, author of *The Ragamuffin Gospel*, describes it this way: "To live by grace means to acknowledge my whole life story, the light side and the dark. In admitting my shadow side I learn who I am and what God's grace means."[3]

Here are the characteristics of these two opposing natures:

FALSE SELF	TRUE SELF
• relies on self	• walks in the Spirit
• idolizes control	• trusts God's sovereignty
• projects an image	• reflects His image
• performs for acceptance	• rests in Christ's approval

The motivations of the false self represent spiritual immaturity, while the motivations of the true self represent spiritual maturity. Living out of the false self—living by the flesh—is all about self; living out of the true self—living by the Spirit—is all about others. And while the characteristics of the false self limit greater self-awareness, the characteristics of the true self promote greater self-awareness.

It is critical we understand there will be no in-depth self-awareness apart from a personal relationship with God. In his book *Prayer: Experiencing Awe and Intimacy with God*, Tim Keller states, "Nothing but prayer will ever reveal you to yourself, because only before God can you see and become your true self."[4]

We can see the truth of Keller's words in the life of Joe DiMaggio, the New York Yankee baseball player. DiMaggio was larger than life in his day. Fans loved him and reporters praised him for his exceptional talent. To add to his notoriety, he married one of the most famous women ever, Marilyn Monroe.

Following his death, it was revealed that DiMaggio had projected an image for eighty-three years that was not true. In *Joe DiMaggio: The Hero's Life,* Richard Cramer tells of the emptiness of Joe's life because of his commitment to "show nothing but a shiny face of his own devising."[5] According to Cramer, DiMaggio masked the truth that he was an egocentric, greedy, selfish man driven by power and money.

Dr. David Benner rightly determines that we are all capable of living such a life of delusion. In *The Gift of Being Yourself* he says, "There can be no true life apart from relationship to God. Therefore, there can be no true self apart from this relationship. The foundation of our identity resides in our life-giving relationship with the Source of Life. Any identity that exists apart from this relationship is an illusion."[6]

Barry was not aware of what he was missing in his life. He was a successful orthopedic surgeon who developed a revolutionary total knee replacement technique. He trained surgeons from around the world to use his procedure.

"During the early years of my medical career I made my work my god," Barry said. He thought he would find complete satisfaction and fulfillment from his practice. But as a result of working too much and making other bad choices, his first marriage failed.

Three years later, Barry married Lynda. Soon after, they became captivated by the lives of another couple. Their marriage had something that Barry's did not.

Fortunately, these two couples started spending time together and became good friends. Barry and Lynda began visiting church with them. Slowly but surely, Barry and Lynda discovered what had been missing in their lives.

In a church service on November 25, 1985, without any prior conversation with each other about what God had been revealing in their hearts, Barry and Lynda committed their lives to Jesus Christ. They were both shocked by and thankful for each other's decision.

This new spiritual awareness began changing the way they lived, what they lived for, and the way they loved others. Becoming a Christ-follower launched Barry's self-awareness journey.

One area that changed immediately was the way he cared for his patients. "For the next twenty years I approached practicing medicine with a different attitude and a greater compassion. I began treating people rather than just diseases," he explained.

At his retirement party from his medical practice of thirty-six years, hundreds of his patients came to tell him how much they loved him.

God used another couple in Barry's life and the compassion of Christ to make him aware that people were more important than tasks. Once God put a servant's heart into Barry, his service didn't stop with retirement. In short order he

- founded the Life Skills Institute at the University of Arkansas Medical School, utilizing volunteers to train senior medical students in non-medical matters and how to incorporate one's spirituality into the practice of medicine;

- helped establish a free medical clinic in the inner city; and

- established an orthopedic team to bolster a surgical teaching ministry in Honduras, resulting in ten to twelve teams a year radically changing the patient care and surgical practices in that country.

Inside-out leaders like Barry long for greater awareness regarding the tendencies of their false self and their true self. In his book *True Self/False Self* Basil Pennington explains, "The core of the false self is the belief that my value depends on what I have, what I can do, and what others think of me."[7]

Leaders who want to hold onto their preferred image of themselves will ignore how adhering to the false self actually becomes a barrier to personal maturity and fulfillment. On the other hand, leaders who desire to cultivate the Spirit-filled qualities of their true self will not only recognize false-self tendencies but also acknowledge them to God and to others.

To experience true fulfillment, leaders must draw humbly upon the presence and power of God for transformation. They will trust the One who created them to help them fully own and take responsibility for both selves.

Paul identified with the challenges of this growth process: "For I know that nothing good dwells in me, that is, in my flesh [false self]. For I have the desire to do what is right, but not the ability to carry it out [apart from the person of the Holy Spirit empowering my true self]" (Romans 7:18).

Nothing in our lives is hidden from God. He knows what we are thinking and what we are feeling. He desires that we follow David's example when he said to the Lord, "God, see what is in my heart. Know what is there. Test me. Know what I'm thinking. See if there's anything in my life you don't like. Help me live in the way that is always right" (Psalm 139:23–24 NIRV).

After seven years Fellowship Bible Church began experiencing rapid, even miraculous growth in numbers of people and changed lives. Some 1,500–2,000 people were attending our worship services. My partners, Bill Parkinson and Robert Lewis, and I were feeling really burned out trying to cover all the needs.

God used a close friend and church member to point out our need for additional staff. With God's help, we added some very gifted people to our team.

I knew I was tired during this period of incessant activity, but I was not aware of the cost to the health of my soul. Self-reliance and working harder, longer, and faster had distracted me from God's presence and power.

My listening skills and ability to be present with those I led both at home and at church were lacking. Unknowingly, I had become too preoccupied with everything I needed to get done while neglecting relational connections. I had no margin in my schedule-packed life to respond to those special Holy Spirit moments and unplanned ministry opportunities.

I could identify with what Ruth Barton, co-founder and president of the Transforming Center, writes in *Strengthening the Soul of Your Leadership*: "It is possible to gain the world of ministry success and lose your own soul in the midst of it all. . . . These days (and maybe every day) there is a real tension between what the human soul needs in order to be truly well and what life in leadership encourages and even requires."[8]

From this experience I became aware of two important leadership lessons:

1. A self-reliant, fast-paced, multi-tasking lifestyle is very seductive. Being in demand can make you feel important, needed, and valuable, but it delivers a false sense of fulfillment.

2. Self-sufficiency keeps you from self-awareness. It distracts you from the One who knows you best and who wants to empower you to become your true self.

So how can a leader become more self-aware? I don't have a recipe for this. Growing in self-awareness is a unique spiritual journey for every leader. It is a process that takes place over time. However, I am pleased to share a few things from my own journey that have been beneficial to me.

First, I simply told the Lord that I longed to understand myself better from the *inside-out*. I needed His help.

Augustine poses a probing question in *Confessions*: "How can you draw close to God when you are far from your own self?" Then he prayed, "Grant, Lord, that I may know myself that I may know Thee."[9]

This journey has been challenging, embarrassing, and fulfilling to me at the same time. I have become aware that defensive people like me are among the least self-aware because they are unwilling to listen to the perceptions of others. They have a greater need to protect an idealized image of themselves. Ouch!

But what I love is that God is changing me—not just my behavior. I know that He has more for me to learn, and I will need His grace to apply what He reveals.

Second, I have pursued an ever-deepening spirit-to-Spirit connection, confident that I cannot advance in self-awareness without a power much greater than my own.

This is the purpose of Paul's prayer from a jail cell in Rome:

> For this reason I bow my knees before the Father, from whom every family in heaven and on earth is named, that according to the riches of his glory he may grant you to be strengthened with power through his Spirit in your inner being, so that Christ may dwell in your hearts through faith—that you, being rooted and grounded in love, may have strength to comprehend with all the saints what is the breadth and length and height and depth, and to know the love of Christ that surpasses knowledge, that you may be filled with all the fullness of God (Ephesians 3:14–19).

Paul did not pray for the external circumstances the Ephesian believers were facing but rather for a growing intimacy with the Holy Spirit. He wanted them to experience an ongoing relational connection with the Holy Spirit's power in their "inner being." He also prayed for an increasing comprehension of the immensity of God's love for them. Our Lord and Savior desires the same for us today.

Personally speaking, this translates to me prioritizing more time to quietly reflect on God's perspective about everything. It is processing my emotions, decision-making, and troublesome relationships in partnership with the Spirit's guidance.

It is yielding to divine empowerment in order to subdue those parts of my leadership that can hurt others, because I am not aware of how they are perceiving me. "'Not by might, nor by power, but by my Spirit,' says the Lord of hosts" (Zechariah 4:6).

In short, to cultivate a growing spirit-to-Spirit connection I must have time for being completely present to the Trinity.

Third, I read and studied numerous books whose authors have served as mentors to me.

When I was growing up I didn't enjoy reading at all. I preferred the playground to the classroom. Fortunately, this preference has changed as I have aged. I have been able to see the incredible value of being mentored by others through reading.

Digesting the wisdom and experiences of others has given me a much better understanding of the language of self-awareness. Emotional intelligence, true self, false self, shadow work, differentiation, and other concepts have provided a helpful framework for me to understand myself with greater confidence.

Aldous Huxley, author of *Jesting Pilate*, wrote, "Every man . . . who knows how to read, has it in his power to magnify himself, to multiply the ways in which he exists, to make his life full, significant, and interesting."[10]

Here is a short list of some good books that expanded my understanding about self-awareness:

- » *The Relational Soul,* by Richard Plass and Jim Cofield

- » *Emotionally Healthy Spirituality,* by Peter Scazzero

- » *The Gift of Being Yourself,* by David G. Benner

- » *Strengthening the Soul of Your Leadership,* by Ruth Haley Barton

- » *The Cure,* by Bill Thrall, Bruce McNicol, and John Lynch

A good leader will take time to explore and reflect on the interior of his or her life with challenging books!

Another way I have been mentored is through the wisdom and support of a small group of men. This group is not just any gathering of men. It is an authentic spiritual community where relationships are characterized by trust, vulnerability, and mutual submission.

We process life together as it happens. We discuss family challenges, health issues, financial matters, vocational concerns, and relational conflicts. It is a confidence-keeping, safe place where men are helping each other see their blind spots.

On one occasion I asked my group to participate in a 360-degree assessment inventory I was taking to gain some self-awareness insights about my leadership. My perceptions of myself and those of my brothers were not the same! Their candid responses were very beneficial to me and I have learned to be grateful for this kind of honest feedback. "Faithful are the wounds of a friend" (Proverbs 27:6).

Self-awareness is a lifelong journey. Here is a list of truths and the threats that undermine each step.

Self-awareness is . . .

① **Not just** having a clear understanding of your strengths **but also** having a clear understanding of your weaknesses.

> **THREAT: When leaders are unwilling to face their insecurities.** *Defensiveness is often their self-protecting response to keep from facing weakness.*

② **Not just** seeking to be fully present to yourself **but also** seeking to be fully present to God and to others.

> **THREAT: When leaders are driven.** *Their hurriedness, busyness, and multi-tasking keep them from being fully present to anyone, including themselves.*

3 Not just being connected to the thoughts in your head **but also** being in touch with the feelings in your heart.

THREAT: When leaders won't allow themselves to feel. *Denial, an inability to identify their feelings, and fear keep their hearts closed off.*

4 Not just being aware of how your emotions affect you **but also** being aware of how your emotions affect those around you.

THREAT: When leaders undervalue emotional intelligence or have little concern about how they come across to others.

5 Not just recognizing a personal blind spot occasionally **but also** inviting others to reveal your blind spots to you.

THREAT: When leaders resist vulnerability. *They lack the emotional strength and humility to benefit from the insights of others.*

6 **Not just** avoiding being controlled by the approval of others **but also** avoiding being controlled by the disapproval of others.

THREAT: When leaders prioritize their image over their substance. *They attempt to manage their perceived feelings of others so much that they give their leadership away.*

7 **Not just** knowing how God wants to use your abilities to bless others **but also** knowing how the gifts of others are needed by you.

THREAT: When leaders depend on self-reliance and self-sufficiency. *They believe it is always easiest to take care of things on their own.*

8 **Not just** through experiencing a miraculous new birth **but also** through experiencing many transformations according to your intimacy with the Trinity.

THREAT: When leaders are lacking solitude in their lives. *Their viewpoint that solitude is non-productive down time could not be farther from the truth. It is the preeminent place for spiritual transformation and empowerment of a leader.*

The road to self-awareness is not easy or quick. ***You have to want it!*** Beware:

- It's easier to rely on yourself than to tell God that you long to become more self-aware.

- It's easier to rely on yourself than to pursue a greater spirit-to-Spirit connection for the power to overcome traits of your personality that cause harm to others.

- It's easier to rely on yourself than to open your heart to be mentored by others.

Author, educator, and activist Parker Palmer shares this warning: "A leader is a person who must take special responsibility for what's going on inside of himself or herself . . . lest the act of leadership creates more harm than good."[11]

Another Leader's Story

by Kris Brossett

Getting arrested and put in prison was the best thing that ever happened to me.

When I was a child I desperately wanted someone to notice me. I was lonely and hurting. My father was addicted to drugs and rarely present. My mother remarried, and my stepfather was abusive. I felt abandoned.

In my desperation I determined to pursue my cousin's way of life. To escape his pain and absent father, he became a gangster. He was on his own. He appeared to be unaffected by his past, so I concluded that following in his footsteps would protect me. Looking back, I can see I was destined to be a gangster.

In sixth grade I got arrested at school for trying to sell some of my stepfather's marijuana to another student. The student snitched on me and my mom found me at the police station, where I was handcuffed to a bench.

Within a few years I joined a gang; my cousin's life became my life. I thought being a gangster would erase my agony, but it only accentuated it. Gangbanging was just another insecurity mask. While it provided a sense of control, it didn't solve my problems. It's a lifestyle full of deception, violence, and betrayal.

At seventeen I got shot and my homies betrayed me; they showed their true colors. My new family, the gang I pledged my life to, wasn't there for me. I realized I couldn't trust anyone and I hated humanity, but the question that kept coming up in my mind was "Am I trustworthy?" I wasn't.

I had worn a mask for so long, I didn't know the real me. I had spent my entire life trying to be like someone else.

I was already running from the law when I got shot. Thank God, I got arrested again. After being sentenced, I was moved to a temporary reception facility in order to determine where I would serve my time. At that facility I met another inmate who knew Jesus. He had a glow about him, and I wanted *the glow*. One evening I surrendered to Jesus in the prison chapel, and my life changed forever.

Following Jesus in prison had its own set of challenges. It was even more difficult when I was paroled. Not only did I have to figure out who I was, but I still had baggage from who I used to be. During this time I met my wife, we had three beautiful children, and I worked a job in construction. Over the years I served at a local church, where I became a lay pastor.

Later something weird started to take place in my heart. A burden developed for the community I grew up in. I didn't know how to process it, but God made sure it was crystal clear—He used my wife! At one point she looked me in the eyes and told me it was time to plant a church. I was terrified but I knew it was true.

Now I was responsible for a ministry, and my insecurities surfaced. In fact, they intensified. I wanted to please God and do well. However, I knew I couldn't. I was afraid of people.

I have since learned that God calls imperfect people to a mission that only He can accomplish. This means every minister will make mistakes. When I did, it crushed me. Every critical email reinforced my inadequacies. What was I to do? The difficulty associated with ministry drove me to my knees. My growth in self-awareness began there.

When God calls a man to a ministry, the ministry is the means He uses to transform him. Ministry is a calling in which God uses a particular individual to display His glory in the world.

Unlike the world, God doesn't prop up peoples' strengths. Instead, He strengthens those who have surrendered to Him. In fact, usefulness is possible only when you're completely available to God in whatever way He wants to use you. This has been the hardest lesson for me to learn and my greatest lesson for self-awareness.

Moses started out an insecure man like me. He was abandoned and betrayed, like me. He was called to a ministry too big for his own good, like me. Also like me, everything about the ministry required his faith. A verse from his story motivates me to pursue greater self-awareness: "And there has not arisen a prophet since in Israel like Moses, whom the Lord knew *face to face*" (Deuteronomy 34:10, emphasis mine).

Do you see what happened? The tender hand of God met the brokenness of His servant. There is no way to know yourself until you know the face of God. God will bring up all your insecurities so that He can mend your wounds. The same God who called Moses is the God I serve. I am sure He is using everything in my life to draw me to Him. When my chief end is to please and glorify God, I can hold everything else with an open hand.

Self-awareness is scary because it requires honesty. It means you must be open to criticism and praise. Without this kind of vulnerability, you'll never be self-aware. If you mask your insecurities instead of turning them over to God, you'll cut yourself off from self-awareness. The more I began to trust God, the more self-aware I became. He has never failed me.

— *KRIS BROSSETT is the lead pastor of Refuge LA in North Hollywood, California.*

"Search me, God, and know my heart; test me and know my anxious thoughts. See if there is any offensive way in me, and lead me in the way everlasting."

— *Psalm 139:23–24 NIV*

Reflect:

» Do you long to understand "you" better?

» If a counselor asked you how self-aware you are, how would you answer?

» What struggles are going on in your heart between your false self and your true self?

» Can you say with confidence what you believe is the purpose of your life?

» Like John the Baptist, are there areas in your life where God must increase and you must decrease?

Record

Which question(s) captured your attention the most? Write down your thoughts, feelings, action steps, and anything else God reveals to your heart.

_____

_____

_____

_____

_____

_____

Remember:

- Leaders' influence—for good or evil, to help others or to hurt them, to draw attention to themselves or to glorify God—is directly related to the depth of their self-awareness.

- Leaders must fully embrace the tendencies of their false selves and their true selves. Such openness and vulnerability are essential to personal transformation.

- It is impossible for leaders to develop a deeper understanding of their true identity apart from a life-giving, personal relationship with the Source of life.

Chapter 2

UNIQUE DESIGN

> *"The question is not what we intended ourselves to be,*
> *but what He intended us to be when He made us."*
> *— C. S. Lewis*

THE FAMILIAR YET COMPELLING STORY of Joseph is captured beautifully for us in Genesis. It is the story of unforgivable human injustice wedded to the unmistakable sovereignty of God. "What man meant for evil God meant for good" is the usual moral of the story. But as we recount his life, look for Joseph's God-given design and how it plays into his destiny.

From the very outset, we learn that Joseph was the favored son of his father. He was an answer to the prayers of his mother, who had been unable to conceive until God "opened her womb" (Genesis 30:22).

Jacob unwisely showed his favoritism to Joseph over his other sons and even made him "a varicolored tunic" (Genesis 37:3 NASB). This special treatment generated great envy and resentment in the hearts of Joseph's brothers.

It didn't help that Joseph interpreted a couple of his dreams to his family, announcing that one day they would all bow down to him. Such boasting was the straw that broke the camel's back. Envy and resentment quickly turned into a plot to murder their arrogant-sounding younger brother. Fortunately, this plot was interrupted by his brother Reuben, who said, "Let us not take his life. . . . [T]hrow him into this pit here in the wilderness" (Genesis 37:21–22). To cover their tracks, Joseph's brothers deceived their father by showing him Joseph's special tunic covered with the blood of an animal.

Joseph was found in the pit, rescued by a caravan of Midianite traders, and sold into slavery in Egypt. He was purchased by Potiphar, an Egyptian officer of Pharaoh. Joseph found favor in the house of Potiphar because "His master saw that the Lord was with him and that the Lord caused all that he did to succeed in his hand" (Genesis 39:3).

Because Joseph was a handsome and well-built slave, Potiphar's wife attempted to seduce him on numerous occasions, but Joseph refused her advances.

One day she grabbed him by his garment and it came off. He fled, leaving his garment behind. This time she became furious. She lied to the servants and to her husband, saying that Joseph had tried to seduce her. Her false accusations resulted in Joseph being thrown into prison. But the prison warden saw his skills and put Joseph in charge of the prison.

After two years in prison, Joseph interpreted a dream for Pharaoh. Pharaoh freed him and chose him to lead Egypt through seven years of plenty and seven years of famine.

God used the famine to bring his brothers to Egypt in search of food. Following a series of interactions with them, Joseph disclosed himself to them and offered forgiveness to his brothers instead of revenge. His family was restored and he provided for all their needs.

His interpretation of his own dream as a young teenager came true. Not only his family members but all of Egypt bowed down to Joseph, a man who enjoyed God's favor.

Did you pick up on the profound connection between Joseph's God-given design and his destiny?

- When we first meet Joseph as a teenager, he was **tending his father's sheep**.

- Potiphar made him **overseer of his house and all his possessions**.

- Joseph found favor with the prison warden, who **put him in charge of all the prisoners**.

- Joseph interpreted Pharaoh's dream and Pharaoh **positioned him to manage his household and all the people of Egypt.**

One thing is perfectly clear about Joseph's design: He was always put in charge! Even on his deathbed he was giving orders and overseeing the disposition of his remains. Joseph's unique calling in life was to manage things for the benefit of others and the glory of God. Repeatedly he was tapped by others to meet a special need using his leadership gifts and abilities. His successful track record in each assignment revealed that he was energized by what he did and that he did it well. God confirmed it. This was his destiny!

Have you discovered your destiny? Discovering my unique God-given design has been an ongoing pursuit for many years.

During my college years I was not sure what I wanted to pursue vocationally. Business school was the right place for my training, but I was not right for it. I made decent grades, looking successful on the outside, but I needed to do some growing up on the inside. I needed to have a better understanding of my unique design from God. At that time I was clueless. I spent a full year in law school after graduation, but I soon learned that wasn't for me either.

But God was faithful to use over thirty years at Fellowship Bible Church for my unique design-learning laboratory. It was in this growing church environment that I was given rich leadership opportunities. Each one began to inform me about my God-given design. For example, I led elder board meetings, negotiated land purchases, provided oversight for multi-million-dollar construction projects, managed staff, discipled small-group leaders, conducted numerous weddings and funerals, and served on our preaching team.

During this period I confirmed that I had a God-given ability for strategic thinking, project management, collaboration, and execution. Using these abilities remains energizing to me to this day.

A moment of significant insight occurred, however, when I realized that years before I had become a Christ-follower, I was organizing, arranging, and managing things. For example, when I was in elementary school I would spend hours rearranging the furniture in my room. Getting everything organized according to my latest layout was satisfying to me. I did not become a Christ follower until high school, but an important principle I have learned is that our natural abilities given to us at conception and our spiritual gifts received from God at conversion should not be viewed as mutually exclusive but rather as complementary. All our gifts and abilities are grace gifts. We did not earn them or deserve them. God gave them to us.

Our spiritual gifts enrich and empower God's original design in our lives. This is not to say that the Designer cannot choose to give a spiritual gift for a special purpose that has nothing to do with His original handiwork in a person's life. However, in most instances that is not the case. The apostle Paul's life serves as an illustration:

> For you have heard of my former manner of life in Judaism, how I used to persecute the church of God beyond measure and tried to destroy it; and I was advancing in Judaism beyond many of my contemporaries among my countrymen, being more extremely zealous for my ancestral traditions. But when God, who had set me apart even from my mother's womb [conception] and called me through His grace, was pleased to reveal His Son in me [conversion] so that I

might preach Him among the Gentiles. (Galatians
1:13–16 NASB)

From conception, Paul's design included a boldness of
personality, outstanding leadership ability, and unusual
oratory skills. Unfortunately, prior to his conversion
he employed his design to persecute the church and to
impress others.

Following his Damascus road conversion, Paul's unique
design did not change, but his heart and the useful
purpose of his design dramatically changed. Now he
was presenting the gospel of Jesus Christ to the Gentiles.
That was his destiny!

In the early 1990s I found myself on a design assessment-
training track. Our leadership at Fellowship wanted to
find a tool to help members better understand their God-
given DNA in order to find their best fit to serve others,
both inside and outside our church. I was certified by
People Management International in their System for
Identifying Motivated Abilities (SIMA) technology and by
Personal Technologies to use their Servants by Design™
assessment instrument. These tools were extraordinarily

beneficial to my design discovery process. This was an "aha" moment for me. God provided me with a new level of clarity about how He had hardwired me to be a blessing to others. As Peter put it, "Each of you should use whatever gift you have received to serve others, as faithful stewards of God's grace in its various forms" (1 Peter 4:10 NIV).

During this season the Lord led me to start a men's discipleship ministry called Kingdom Builders. I invited four to six men each year to join me weekly, early in the morning, at my house. Our purpose was to pursue a deeper understanding of our God-given design and how to employ it for the benefit of others and the glory of God.

I enjoyed these energizing groups for twelve years. We forged meaningful friendships, and the spiritual fruitfulness of our lives soared. I honestly don't know who helped whom more. Was God using me to disciple these men or was He using these men to disciple me? Most probably it was a little of both.

One of the exercises we did together involved helping each other, through prayer and counsel, to identify

a single word that best described each man's God-
given design. That word had to strike a chord in each
man's heart regarding God's workmanship in his life.
Gatekeeper, networker, coach, guide, influencer, catalyzer,
and others emerged. This was an exciting and incredibly
bonding exercise to work through as a team.

On one occasion I shared that I believed my word was
encourager. Immediately one of the men disagreed,
saying that while being an encourager was certainly
true of me, it didn't capture a full expression of my
leadership. Then he offered the word *builder,* stating it
felt stronger to him and more completely described how
God had used me for years. The other men in the group
affirmed this description and ultimately I did as well. So
"Bill the Builder" it was.

But my design understanding continued to grow. In
every new season of life, I felt God was revealing fresh
nuances to me about my unique design.

On my sixtieth birthday something happened that I will
never forget. All my adult children and their families
came to our house for a birthday dinner. After dinner

I was completely caught off guard by what took place. Representing his sister, his brother, their spouses, and all my grandchildren, my oldest son, Bill, stood and said he had something to share. Then he presented me with a beautifully framed picture with sixty reasons why they all loved me. Each statement was signed by the adult or child who had made it. My heart was so full as they read these to me. What a treasure!

But that wasn't all. Bill handed me another present. I opened it and found a first-class volleyball signed by all of them. All eyes were on me. Then he said, "This volleyball is a symbol of who you are to us. You are a 'setter,' Dad. God designed you to set other people up to win. We have all experienced this from you."

With tears in my eyes, I was speechless. Needless to say, since that night my single-word description has been *setter*. I do love helping people win in their lives for the glory of God. In my present season of life, God is using my design to help church planters win. It's a great fit for a setter!

Tad, a chairman and CEO of an insurance company and a member of a Kingdom Builder group, called me one day to see if I could attend a meeting with him and two other business leaders to discuss a new ministry idea. All three of these men were the entrepreneurial leaders of their companies, so I knew this would be a blast. It was!

They shared their idea of beginning a mentoring ministry for young business leaders. Their plan was to share lessons God had taught them from failure and success about corporate leadership, balancing family and work, church involvement, and being faithful examples for Christ in their business dealings. Appropriately, they named their ministry "KingdomCorp."

Tad told me, "I have prayed about this and talked to you for two years regarding how God wanted to use my unique design in the lives of others. I am absolutely certain this is it."

With the Lord's help Tad had made a significant discovery. He had identified not only a personal ministry to benefit others but also a single-word description of his God-given design—*influencer*. He has been faithfully leading these mentoring groups and "influencing" young entrepreneurs for thirteen years.

"It has been the joy of my life to watch these men discover greater clarity about the direction of their lives, to lead their wives and children spiritually, to improve their witness for Christ by changing their business priorities, and to lock arms together to help one another succeed," explained Tad.

David looked at God's involvement in each person's unique design and said, "For you formed my inward parts; you knitted me together in my mother's womb. I praise you, for I am fearfully and wonderfully made. Wonderful are your works; my soul knows it very well" (Psalm 139:13–14). You are "fearfully and wonderfully made." You have been given a one-of-a-kind, special design from God. No one can do what you can do in precisely the same way.

"In your book were written, every one of them, the days that were formed for me, when as yet there was none of them" (Psalm 139:16). David saw God's design involvement not only in the womb but also in the destiny of his life.

Another example of this design-to-destiny connection

is seen in the life of Jeremiah. It blows my mind! Read this carefully: "Now the word of the Lord came to me, saying, 'Before I formed you in the womb I knew you, and before you were born I consecrated you; I appointed you a prophet to the nations'" (Jeremiah 1:4–5). God was intentionally involved in Jeremiah's design-to-destiny connection even before He formed him in the womb. He has a plan and purpose for our lives as well.

How do leaders develop a deeper understanding of their God-given design? How can the connection between a person's design and his or her destiny be identified? God has been teaching me four perspectives on my design discovery journey. This is an ongoing process for me. I believe it will be for you as well.

First, **God is the Creator and Owner of every person's design.** The Parable of Talents in Matthew 25:14–30 communicates this truth.

In this parable a certain master gives three servants a specific amount of money, called a talent, to invest or manage for him. Then he leaves on a long journey. Upon his return he discovers that two servants have been faithful but one unfaithful in the stewardship of what was entrusted to them. Two servants doubled what was given to them, but one misused what he received by burying it in the ground.

Our story is similar. God is our CEO. We are His servants. He has created and entrusted to each person a unique, one-of-a-kind mix of gifts and abilities. We are to invest them for His glory and the blessing of others. Like the master in the parable, one day our Master will return and we will give an account for our stewardship. As Paul states, "For we must all appear before the judgment seat of Christ, so that each one may receive what is due for what he has done in the body, whether good or evil" (2 Corinthians 5:10). C. S. Lewis once observed, "The more we let God take over, the more truly ourselves we become because He made us."[12]

> For by him all things were created, in heaven and on earth, visible and invisible. . . . [A]ll things were created through him and for him. And he is before all things, and in him all things hold together. (Colossians 1:16–17)

Second, **God rewards faithfulness, not giftedness.**

Read these words from the same parable: "To one he gave five talents, to another two, to another one, to each according to his ability. Then he went away" (Matthew 25:15). Jesus explained the reason one servant is entrusted with five talents, another with two talents, and a third servant with one: "to each according to his [own] ability."

The abilities of each servant have a unique capacity. The master does not ask the one-talent servant to multitask, because this would overwhelm him. Nor does he underutilize the five-talent servant by entrusting him with just one talent. Rather, the master seeks to maximize the contributions of each servant.

Further, it is notable that both the five-talent servant and the two-talent servant receive the identical commendation from their master. Twice he repeats the same phrase: "Well done, good and faithful slave. You were faithful with a few things, I will put you in charge of many things; enter into the joy of your master" (Matthew 25:21, 23 NASB).

God values and rewards faithfulness in the use of our design, not just the magnitude of our giftedness.

Take Helen, for example. She was a kind, thoughtful single parent who loved Jesus. Everyone on our church staff loved her. Actually, everyone who met her loved her.

Helen wasn't trained as a bookkeeper and she never had the opportunity to attend college, but she was a faithful employee. She prided herself in working hard to keep our church's financial records accurate to the penny, spending hours to find even the smallest error.

This faithful widow never forgot to send you a card on your birthday, nor did she miss mailing or delivering a card or small gift to each of your children on their birthdays. And she prayed for you constantly.

It was an honor to lead Helen Richards's funeral service. This caring friend and loyal, behind-the-scenes worker led a simple life that had a profound witness for Jesus Christ. Her legacy was not about her training or her abilities; it was about her faithfulness. I am certain that when she met Jesus face to face, He rewarded her with "Well done, good and faithful slave. You were faithful with a few things, I will put you in charge of many things; enter into the joy of your master" (Matthew 25:21 NASB). Third, **God does not want us to compare.**

In our society, comparison is rampant. We compare cars, houses, incomes, job titles, vacations, size of churches, business growth, appearances, and leadership abilities. You name it—we compare it.

Comparison, however, is dangerous. It promotes jealousy, conflict, and disunity. It drains leaders' energy and distracts them from doing what they were uniquely made to do. It can even result in what I call design dissatisfaction.

Design dissatisfaction is feeling that you do not measure up to the task or that someone else would be a better choice. At one point in his life, Moses suffered from this form of comparison.

After Moses's four decades in the wilderness, God spoke to him from a burning bush: "Come, I will send you to Pharaoh that you may bring my people, the children of Israel, out of Egypt" (Exodus 3:10).

Moses had attempted to do this on his own forty years earlier and failed miserably. God now confirmed to him that He would empower him to deliver His people.

His calling and the purpose of his life are clearly stated. Moses's unique design and destiny were to be the deliverer God had made him to be. Somewhat surprisingly, Moses struggled, doubted, complained, and even offered all kinds of excuses as to why he was inadequate for the task.

Who am I? Who shall I say sent me? What if they don't believe me? Lord, You know I'm not a good communicator. Please send someone else. Even though God promised to be with Moses and answered every excuse, he struggled with design dissatisfaction.

It took time for Moses to understand that the Designer never asks you to do what He has not designed and empowered you to do. In fact, to reject your unique design in any way is to reject the Designer and His purpose for your life. "But who are you, O man, to answer back to God? Will what is molded say to its molder, 'Why have you made me like this?'" (Romans 9:20).

The world's plan is based upon comparison. It promotes sameness. God's plan is based upon each person being "fearfully and wonderfully made." It promotes uniqueness.

While some leaders are more visible and others are behind the scenes, from God's perspective there are no insignificant contributions. Every person has a role to play according to his or her God-given design. "As it is, there are many parts, yet one body. The eye cannot say to the hand, 'I have no need of you,' nor again the head to the feet, 'I have no need of you.' On the contrary, the parts of the body that seem to be weaker are indispensable" (1 Corinthians 12:20–22).

Fourth, **God desires for us to understand our unique design and destiny.**

Here are some practical tips to consider:

⁓ *Take advantage of assessment tools.*

Earlier I mentioned how these resources had helped me in my design discovery journey. While I have used several, the Servants by Design™ inventory at www.youruniquedesign.com has benefitted me the most.

If you utilize more than one assessment tool, place them side by side and study them carefully to see where they overlap in confirming your design strengths or where a repeated pattern or theme emerges. This is a good indicator of your sweet spot.

∼ *Pursue honest feedback from others.*

"Without counsel plans fail, but with many advisers they succeed" (Proverbs 15:22). Everyone has blind spots. All leaders need a community of those who know them best to confirm or challenge their conclusions about their unique design. If married, be sure to include your spouse. He or she likely knows you better than anyone.

Very simply, together is better than alone when seeking clarity about your design and your destiny.

∼ *Read books to stimulate your thinking.*

Here is a short list that helped me:

- *The Call,* by Os Guiness

- *Let Your Life Speak,* by Parker Palmer

- *Experiencing God,* by Henry Blackaby, Richard Blackaby, and Claude King

- *Living the Life That You Were Meant to Live,* by Tom Patterson

- *The Eighth Habit,* by Stephen R. Covey

- *Strengths Based Leadership,* by Tom Rath and Barry Conchie

- *Freed to Be Me: A Servant by Design,* by Dr. Robert S. Maris and Anna Maris Kirkes

Remember: an inside-out leader is a lifelong learner. Build a self-knowledge library.

⌒ *Carve out some time for solitude.*

Every person can benefit from assessments, honest feedback, and reading, but everything must be filtered at a heart level in the presence of God.

Henry Nouwen offers these thoughts about the value of solitude:

We enter into solitude first of all to meet our Lord and to be with Him and Him alone. . . . Only in the context of grace can we face our sin; only in the place of healing do we dare to show our wounds; only with single-minded attention to Christ can we give up our clinging fears and face our own true nature. . . . It is a place where Christ remodels us in his own image and frees us from the victimizing compulsions of the world.[13]

The prophet Elijah's experience is a case in point. After he had miraculously defeated the prophets of Baal on Mount Carmel, Queen Jezebel threatened to take his life. Terrified, Elijah fled into the desert. Angels of the Lord provided for his needs. Then after a lengthy trip, he found himself in the solitude of a cave.

And behold, the Lord passed by, and a great and strong wind tore the mountains and broke in pieces the rocks before the Lord, but the Lord was not in the wind. And after the wind an earthquake, but the Lord was not in the earthquake. And after the earthquake a fire, but the Lord was not in the fire. And after the fire the sound of a low whisper. And when Elijah heard it, he wrapped his face in his cloak and went out and stood at the entrance of the cave. And behold, there came a voice to him. (1 Kings 19:11–13)

The Lord was not in the powerful wind, the earthquake, or the fire but rather in the sound of a low whisper. In the solitude of a cave, in the presence of the Lord, Elijah discovered a fresh sense of clarity and direction for the use of his God-given design.

The same is true for you and me. Solitude provides the undistracted space for God to speak to us about our lives. "Let all that I am wait quietly before God, for my hope is in Him" (Psalm 62:5 NLT). Do not rush by the possibility of God communicating heart to heart with you without any effort on your part, save listening.

In addition, here are some questions to ponder in God's presence:

- What do I love to do that energizes me?

- What cause, people group, or need am I passionate about?

- Where do I see God at work? Is there a need for my design?

- Looking back over my life, what did I consistently do that blessed others the most?

- Unsolicited, what have people told me I am good at doing?

Don't just answer these questions in your head. You are not trying to discover something on your own. You are pursuing to "know that you know" your God-given design at a heart level. It is when you can say to yourself, "I am made for this!"

"For we are his workmanship, created in Christ Jesus for good works, which God prepared beforehand, that we should walk in them" (Ephesians 2:10). Simply put, understanding God's design-to-destiny question in your life means knowing who you are, being who you are, living who you are, and employing who you are in meaningful ways for the glory of God and the benefit of others.

Another Leader's Story

by Thien Doan

Finding your unique design isn't as simple as discovering what you are best at doing.

I certainly believed the scripture that each person is "His workmanship," a special masterpiece or a one-of-a-kind poem of grace (Ephesians 2:10). My problem was that when I looked for what I was best at, I couldn't find it, nor has any one thing ever held my interest for very long.

If you put me in a room with my peers, you would find that I am not the smartest, the most talented, the best communicator, the best leader, or frankly the best anything.

Still, I know I am not the only person who has ever felt this way. Scott Adams, creator of the Dilbert comic strip, admits that he is not the best artist, funniest person, or best writer in his field. So how has Dilbert become the most successful and most syndicated comic strip in history?

Adams calls it "talent stacking" or "skills stacking." Like me, he does not have one singular talent that sets him above his competition. Rather, his unique stack of individual skills has contributed to his success.

Scott relates, "When you add in my ordinary business skills, my strong work ethic, my risk tolerance, and my reasonably good sense of humor, I'm fairly unique. And in this case that uniqueness has commercial value."[14] The lesson from Adams's life, to me, is that the whole is greater than the sum of its parts.

This concept of a "skill stack" has encouraged me. It has permitted me to think more broadly about my unique design. In fact, I am best known for my commitment and hard-headed tenacity to accomplish the task at hand. I now realize that my design includes a blend of skills, talents, and experiences as well as these personality traits. When I understand what's in my stack of individual skills and experiences, I can find my greatest contribution to the world. All of these are special gifts from the Lord.

God is purposeful and intentional in how He created each of us. We are not mistakes. God didn't create us by throwing random spare parts together. No, we are indeed one-of-a-kind masterpieces designed for a divine and specific assignment. He has made us the unique solution to accomplish this for Him. Comparison promotes sameness and is opposed to God's plan of uniqueness. We are "fearfully and wonderfully made" by Him (Psalm 139:14).

I encourage you to discover and pursue God's plans for your life. In doing so, you will find out that God created you to be the best in the world for your assignment. And along the way, He will get the glory.

— THIEN DOAN is lead pastor of
City Lights Church in Orange County, California.

What About You?

~

"Search me, God, and know my heart; test me and know my anxious thoughts. See if there is any offensive way in me, and lead me in the way everlasting."

— *Psalm 139:23–24 NIV*

Reflect

» What steps could you take to come to a greater clarity about your God-given design?

» What energizes you and what depletes you?

» Have you experienced a moment when you said to yourself, "I know in my heart that I am made for this"?

» What was it about this moment that was inspiring and fulfilling to you?

» Are you willing to ask a couple of your closest friends and, if married, your spouse to tell you what they believe is your design?

» When have they seen God using you to bless others?

» Can you think of a single word or short phrase that captures the essence of the real you?

Record:

Write down your thoughts, feelings, action steps, questions, and anything else God reveals to your heart.

_____

_____

_____

_____

_____

_____

Remember

- All leaders are "fearfully and wonderfully made." They have each been given a unique design, and discovering their design contributes to a greater understanding of their destiny.

- The special gifts and abilities a leader has received are to be used for the benefit of others and the glory of the Designer. This approach is the key to personal fulfillment! It is also a reminder that life is not about you and me.

- God rewards leaders' faithfulness in the use of their design, not the extent of their giftedness.

Chapter 3

CHARACTER BEFORE
REPUTATION

*"If I take care of my character,
my reputation will take care of me."*
- Dwight L. Moody

TWO WEEKS AFTER HIS TWENTIETH
birthday, William Wilberforce was elected to the
British Parliament. Early in his political career, he knew
his mission. In his diary he wrote, "Almighty God has
set before me two 'Great Objects': the suppression of
the slave trade and the Reformation of Manners."[15]
The subject of the first "object" is self-explanatory; the
second, "Manners," is a bit confusing. By manners he
was referring to a host of social ills including alcoholism,
child labor abuses, and the sexual trafficking of women.

After eighteen grueling years, characterized by one discouraging defeat after another, Wilberforce finally achieved victory in 1807 when he and other abolitionists succeeded in outlawing the slave trade in Great Britain.

What guided this extraordinary leader? What kind of man would choose to pursue such a difficult road? The answer? He was a man of impeccable character.

Wilberforce's inner spiritual conviction propelled him in spite of intense opposition, including threats on his life. He understood that external reputation did not shape internal character. He valued substance over image. He was intent on pleasing the "Audience of One" over the applause of the crowd. Wilberforce exemplified Oswald Chambers's definition of character: "Character in a saint means the disposition of Jesus Christ persistently manifested."[16]

In short, his leadership flowed from the *inside-out*, manifesting the disposition of Jesus. Wilberforce understood before he ever began that his cause would not succeed without the supernatural help of his Lord and Savior, Jesus Christ. God worked in and through him not only to change the culture in Britain but also to influence culture around the world.

Most leaders sense the tension that exists between leading from character or leading from a desire to protect their reputations. David Brooks concludes in *The Road to Character* that "we have shifted from a culture of self-effacement to a culture of display, from a world in which we cultivated restraint, humility, and moral virtues to one in which the measure of our worth, by our own and others' estimation, lies primarily in the realm of self-presentation and professional accomplishment."[17]

Inside-out leaders, however, understand that image is nothing more than who people think you are, while character is who God knows you are.

In the account of God's selection of David as king of Israel, we are reminded of our tendency to look at the outer appearance or image of someone instead of the heart or the core of his or her character. In 1 Samuel 16, Samuel thought that surely Eliab, Jesse's oldest son and one of Saul's warriors, was God's selection to become king. "But the LORD said to Samuel, 'Do not look on his appearance, or on the height of his stature, because I have rejected him. For the LORD sees not as man sees: man looks on the outward appearance, but the LORD looks on the heart'" (1 Samuel 16:7).

The next two sons were also Saul's warriors, but neither of them was chosen. Jesse presented seven of his sons, from oldest to youngest, before Samuel. Not one of them was selected.

Finally, Samuel asked Jesse, "Are these all the sons you have?" (1 Samuel 16:11 NLT). And he replied, in essence, "No, there is the youngest, least significant son taking care of sheep." David was chosen because God said he was "a man after my heart, who will do all my will" (Acts 13:22).

On one hand, Christian leaders want to look good and be approved by others. But on the other hand, they will have to make some decisions, as those Wilberforce had to make, that will not be popular and will result in conflict.

In my life there have been many instances when I wanted to avoid conflict as a leader, and yet the Holy

Spirit would not allow me to escape from wrestling with the spiritual convictions of my heart. Such occasions represent the struggle between leading from a Christ-centered character versus refusing to deal with an issue in order to maintain and protect my image.

Carolyn and I have been married for forty-seven years. Our relationship is stronger, deeper, and richer now than ever before. She is a wonderful wife, life partner, and friend.

I have not always handled conflict well in our relationship. In the early years of our marriage I lacked both the skills and the emotional maturity to be a leader in this area. I didn't want to hurt Carolyn's feelings, but I often did so because of my responses to our disagreements.

On many occasions I would withdraw from her emotionally and become passive. In other instances I would argue that I didn't feel respected by her, attempting to place blame on her. Neither of these is a good approach to conflict resolution.

When I should have been embracing the conflict and leading us to a resolution through mutual understanding, I was retreating as a leader. I was avoiding vulnerability and the discomfort of emotional controversy and trying to protect myself. These responses exposed a character flaw in my heart that I needed to address.

My character development has been shaped and bolstered by a growing intimacy with Jesus and the power of the Holy Spirit. God has used significant relationships with other men to transform my character through mutual accountability. At critical turning points, I have sought the wisdom and experience of Christian counselors to guide my journey. Each one of these has helped me pursue greater integrity between my character and my conduct.

The point is clear—the manner in which a leader handles conflict reveals the character of his or her heart. The character of the leader's heart reveals in whom or in what the leader places his or her trust. "Above all else, guard your heart, for everything you do flows from it" (Proverbs 4:23 NIV).

The apostle Paul is a great example of Jesus launching a character development process in a leader. Paul's Damascus road experience changed everything. Prior to his confrontation with Jesus, Paul was all about his reputation and image. Following that encounter, he considered reputation and image "rubbish," as he stated in the following passage:

> If anyone else thinks he has reasons for confidence in the flesh, I have more: circumcised on the eighth day, of the people of Israel, of the tribe of Benjamin, a Hebrew of Hebrews; as to the law, a Pharisee; as for zeal, a persecutor of the church; as to righteousness under the law, blameless. But whatever gain I had, I counted as loss for the sake of Christ. Indeed, I count everything as loss because of the surpassing worth of knowing Christ Jesus my Lord. For His sake I have suffered the loss of all things and count them as rubbish, in order that I may gain Christ. (Philippians 3:4–8)

Paul had learned that character development was an ongoing, growing process. "Not that I have already obtained all this, or am already perfect, but I press on to make it my own, because Christ Jesus has made me his own" (Philippians 3:12).

In the first season of Paul's life he relied heavily on his persona, his heritage, and his blameless reputation before men he sought to please. Suddenly all of this was re-ordered; he was transformed from persecutor of the church to presenter of the gospel. A new leadership paradigm emerged. Character on the inside became more important to Paul than reputation on the outside! He became an *inside-out* leader.

Paul wrote thirteen of the twenty-seven books of the New Testament. What a legacy he left—all because God had transformed his character!

Christlike character formation is an ongoing process of dependency on Jesus for our sufficiency. No one ever "arrives." The motivation to press on comes from the magnitude of His immense love for us. He has purchased us with His death at Calvary. Christ Jesus has made us His own.

As with Paul, our conversion launches the process of Christlike character development.

It is a startling statement, but we cannot change our character. We can perform or act a certain way, but there will be no real change without complete surrender to God. The third person of the Trinity, the Holy Spirit, is our Helper, who dwells in us to build the character of Christ over time.

While there is one spiritual conversion, there are multiple opportunities for character transformation in our lives. Personally, coming to know Jesus was miraculous and life changing for me. God's amazing grace made me feel loved! I knew I had become a child of God. I understood that He would never leave me or forsake me.

At the same time I was still a newborn, spiritually speaking. I needed to grow up. A friend invited me to join a Bible study on the book of Romans. Coincidentally, I entered the study in the seventh chapter. Paul's words described me perfectly: "For I have the desire to do what is right, but not the ability to carry it out" (Romans 7:18).

I was in Christ but not mature in Christ. Over time my perspective about life began to change. The Scriptures began to make sense to me. A new kind of character was beginning to emerge in me.

I was learning that biblical information did not automatically equal character transformation. The Pharisees had plenty of information and were proud of it, but Jesus said to them, "Woe to you, Scribes and Pharisees, hypocrites! For you are like whitewashed tombs, which outwardly appear beautiful, but within are full of dead people's bones and all uncleanness" (Matthew 23:27).

Jesus was telling the Pharisees that their outward public image and conduct appeared holy but that their inward private character was sinful. He bluntly told them that they modeled knowing information without experiencing transformation. The Pharisees were image-driven leaders. They prayed to be heard and seen. They had knowledge, but they lacked heart-level character transformation.

How do we progress from information to transformation? In my life God has used suffering more than anything else to give me the opportunity for personal transformation, maturation, and character development.

My greatest growth has come when I painfully realize a gap between my dreams and desires compared to reality. There are many areas common to all where these gaps show up. Perhaps you have experienced in the past or are currently facing one or more of life's unexpected gaps:

- unfulfilled purpose or meaning in your profession

- struggles in your marriage

- serious or life-threatening health issues

- conflicts with family members or friends

- broken relationships with a child

- financial stress

- spiritual challenges or disappointment

In each of these gaps you can experience deep feelings of disappointment and hurt and find yourself asking "Why me?" questions.

Here are a few gaps I have experienced:

- The divorce of my parents when I was five years old was not what I had hoped. As a child, I couldn't really understand their separation. I just wished that my mom and dad were together.

- I was totally blindsided when my wife's cancer was discovered twenty-three years ago. I felt numb, and I experienced fear and a sense of helplessness.

- I have had many painful relational conflicts in my faith journey that were completely unanticipated. Some were resolved. Others could not be resolved. I wanted so badly to be able to repair and restore them, but I could not.

- My father's sudden death at age fifty-nine created a huge gap between what I had hoped for and my reality.

All these events were completely beyond my control. In each one my character was being challenged. Could I truly trust God for everything?

We can choose one of two responses to life's gaps—to be reactive or to be receptive.

REACTIVE	RECEPTIVE
More <u>self-reliant</u>, or an "I'll take care of it" attitude	More <u>surrendered</u>, or a "less of me, more of God" attitude

To be honest, I have often found myself in both camps. It is the same warfare Paul describes in Galatians 5:16–17 between the reactive flesh and the receptive Spirit.

On many occasions my reactive responses have included

- » obsessive analysis

- » anxiety

- » fear

- » a desire to control

- » blaming others

- » judging

- » complaining

Please tell me you can identify with me!

In other words, there is no surrender, no "less of me and more of God" in these reactions. My reactive responses have never put the glory of God on display—not a single time.

A heart-level transformation process began in me when I became convicted and more broken about how offensive these reactions were to God's unconditional love and undeserved faithfulness. As this happened, my perceptions about the purposes of suffering, disappointment, and gaps began to change.

In his book *Just This: Prompts and Practices for Contemplation* Richard Rohr explains, "Sooner or later, life is going to lead us . . . into a situation that we can't fix, can't control, and can't explain or understand. That's where transformation most quickly happens. That's when we're uniquely in the hands of God. It's God's Waiting Room! Suffering is the only force strong enough to destabilize the imperial ego."[18]

God was developing my character. He wanted me to become more receptive to gaps. He was revealing to me three truths I am seeking to integrate into my head and heart.

1. Gaps are God's invitation to awaken us to our need for close communion with Him.

Gaps reveal that we are not made to be adequate for life's challenges on our own. When you and I are receptive to gaps, they cultivate a greater awareness of God's presence and power both in us and around us.

Paul prayed three times regarding the removal of his thorn in the flesh. The answer was no. Why? Because God's "grace is sufficient . . . for [His] power is perfected in weakness" (2 Corinthians 12:9 NASB).

I am convinced that Paul's thorn, or his gap, was a spiritual asset God was using to awaken and invite him into a deeper trust relationship that provided even greater power for his leadership.

2. "Gaps" are our greatest opportunities for heart-level transformation and character development.

This truth builds on the first. Once we realize our inadequacies and pursue closer communion with God, we will have fresh opportunities for greater self-awareness and wholeness as Christ-followers.

Success tends to make us arrogant and self-reliant and forgetful of our need for Christ. But in reality, total dependence on Jesus is the most powerful position of all.

Saint Augustine said, "In my deepest wound I saw Your

glory, and it dazzled me."[19] Our greatest wound is an opportunity for our greatest transformation.

3. "Gaps" are privileged moments for putting God's glory on display.

Life is not about you and me. Life is about Him!

How we respond to gaps, to differences between what we hope for and what actually happens, reveals the condition of our character.

Another Leader's Journey
by Jeff Lawrence

The path to becoming an inside-out leader is a lifelong journey. None of us perfectly navigate the terrain, and there are no shortcuts along the way. There are moments, however, that quicken our pace and expedite our learning. These growth spurts are often connected to personal seasons of difficulty or trial.

In my experience the most intense leadership lesson I've learned came from my decision to resign as lead pastor at a church I loved. That decision was one of the most excruciating moments of my life as a leader. The ministry I had labored over and prayed over seemed to be coming undone.

After several years of serving this church family, I reached an impasse with the elders. As a pastor, I had a deep conviction about the kind of community the church should be. The gospel frees us to live in authentic relationships where we share our very lives with one another. Though I tried for several years to bring about this kind of community, I was unsuccessful.

Internally, my heart was in a game of emotional tug-of-war. On one side, the ministry was doing well. We were growing numerically as a church. More people were coming to Christ each year. Disciples were being made. Our ministry programs were thriving. We were making a difference in our city as we served the community at large. On the other side, our leadership team was unhealthy and had always been a battle.

It came down to a matter of stewardship. How did I want to steward my time and energy over the next five years? For my health, family, ministry, and long-term faithfulness to God, I needed to make a change. I could not sacrifice the call of the gospel to authentic community without losing my heart.

I was faced with a difficult choice. In many ways, walking away felt like failure, especially since I struggle with being a bit of an approval junkie. When your significance is tied to your performance, it seems nearly impossible to admit that you can't bring about the results you want. I had to face my feelings of failure (Where did I go wrong?), disappointment (It wasn't supposed to end this way!), regret (I never should have come here!), anger (Who do they think they are?), and self-righteousness (Why won't they just do what the Bible says?). Still, I remain convinced that the decision, as hard as it was, was the right one.

In time I came to realize that some of those feelings were exaggerated and reactive. I learned to turn down the volume on those false voices in my heart and turn up the volume of the gospel voice that speaks both grace and truth. God used the turmoil of that decision as a crucible of character formation in me. I needed to surrender some of my expectations. I needed to learn to be more receptive to God's grace, God's rest, and God's plans. I needed Christ formed in me.

Where character exists, conviction insists and courage acts. All three are necessary in leadership. In a time of tough decision, leaders must rely on character to find the conviction and courage needed for the moment. Character trusts in the sovereignty of God. Character plays the long game, knowing that God will sort things out in the end.

That season, and many since, have continued to increase my confidence that God is both trustworthy and good. Alongside many who have gone before me, I can say, "We rejoice in our sufferings, knowing that suffering produces endurance, and endurance produces character, and character produces hope, and hope does not put us to shame, because God's love has been poured into our hearts through the Holy Spirit who has been given to us" (Romans 5:3–5).

— JEFF LAWRENCE is lead pastor of Redemption Church in Edmond, Oklahoma.

What About You?

~

"Search me, God, and know my heart; test me and know my anxious thoughts. See if there is any offensive way in me, and lead me in the way everlasting."

— *Psalm 139:23–24 NIV*

Reflect

» Do you have an inordinate need to have the approval of others?

» What are some of the gaps you have experienced in your life?

» How did these make you feel?

» What was your response to them?

» How has God shaped your character through suffering or unmet expectations?

» Are you willing to trust God by asking yourself, "What is God wanting to teach me through this unwanted circumstance?"

Record:

Write down your thoughts, feelings, action steps, questions, and anything else God reveals to your heart.

_____

_____

_____

_____

_____

_____

Remember:

- God values leaders' character on the inside more than their image or appearance on the outside.

- Gaps are differences between what a leader desired to happen and what actually occurred. They represent significant opportunities for heart-level transformation.

- Leaders' responses to gaps reveal the character of their hearts and the state of their union with Jesus Christ.

Chapter 4

"TEAM OVER ME"

~

"Leadership is not a solo sport, but a team sport."
- George Barna

F OR SIX MINUTES, TEAMWORK AND perseverance captured the world's attention. The finals of the regatta "took place in the Berlin suburb of Grunau in front of Adolf Hitler and 75,000 fans screaming for the Third Reich."[20] The Germans were anticipating another victory to celebrate their supremacy.

But a rowing crew from the University of Washington, representing the United States in the 1936 Olympics, overcame all odds. They "had been rowing together for less than five months."[21] All were from working- or middle-class families, not your typical rowing team members. They had traveled in third-class accommodations on the SS *Manhattan*. A couple of the men caught serious colds on the voyage across the Atlantic and were not at full strength.

The Americans began the race in their typical fashion with a slow start in the *Huskie Clipper*. Then, with less than three hundred meters to go, "[e]mploying near perfect technique and synchronization,"[22] the nine-man team pulled even with the Germans and the Italians. The three boats matched each other stroke for stroke toward the finish line.

As they crossed the finish line together, the rowers could not tell who had won. The men in all three boats collapsed from exhaustion.

Then came the announcement: "USA 6:25:4, Italy 6:26:0, Germany 6:26:4." Only a single second separated all three boats in what sports writer Grantland Rice described as "the 'high spot' of the 1936 Olympics."[23]

On that day a unique group of college kids worked together in near-perfect unity. They had learned from hours of practice that their team power was much greater than their individual strength. They achieved athletic greatness together and were awarded Olympic gold medals.

George Pocock, the highly regarded designer and builder of the *Huskie Clipper*, offered these thought-provoking words about team: "Where is the spiritual value in rowing? . . . [T]he losing of self entirely to the cooperative effort of the crew as a whole."[24]

Pocock's definition of teamwork is different from ones used by companies, such as "We value teamwork" or "We are organized in teams." Those phrases are more organizational in nature, while the emphasis in this chapter, like Pocock's, is more relational in nature. By *team* I mean a deeply held conviction or value that a group of people embrace to guide their relationships.

Those who value team

- prefer the complementary skills and abilities of others over going it alone,

- listen to the perspective and opinions of others when making important decisions,

- understand that a team protects a company or a congregation from one-sided error,

- believe that pursuing multiple insights moves leadership closer to understanding the mind of Christ, and

- comprehend that team is a virtue that enables teamwork.

Tim Keller confirms this same idea when talking about the value of corporate prayer: "By praying with friends, you will be able to hear and see facets of Jesus that you have not yet perceived."[25]

Team is leadership from the *inside-out*. Peter Drucker, the father of modern management, believed that "All work is for a team. No individual has the temperament and the skill to do every job. The purpose of team is to make strengths productive and weakness irrelevant."[26]

The Bible makes it clear that leadership is not a one-man show. Jethro, Moses's father-in-law, gave this sage advice in Exodus 18:

> It came about the next day that Moses sat to judge the people, and the people stood about Moses from the morning until the evening. Now when Moses' father-in-law saw all that he was doing for the people, he said, "What is this thing that you are doing for the people? Why do you alone sit as judge and all the people stand about you from morning until evening? . . . The thing that you are doing is not good. You will surely wear out, both yourself and these people who are with you, for the task is too heavy for you; you cannot do it alone. Now listen to me: I will give you counsel, and God be with you. . . . [Y]ou shall select out of all the people able men who fear God, men of truth, those who hate dishonest gain; and you shall place these over them as leaders of thousands, of hundreds, of fifties and of tens. Let them judge the people at all times; and let it be that every major dispute they will bring to you, but every minor dispute they themselves will judge. So it will be easier for you,

and they will bear the burden with you." (Exodus 18:13–14, 17–22 NASB)

Moses was wearing out and the people's needs were not being met. The weight of leadership and scope of the nation's expectations in the desert were crushing. Moses desperately needed other qualified leaders or teammates with complementary gifts and abilities to effectively care for this congregation estimated at two million people.

"Able men who feared God, men of truth, those who hated dishonest gain" were chosen. According to their ability, some led thousands, others hundreds; still others led groups of fifty and ten. They were to judge minor disputes, and Moses was to deal with major issues.

No single leader, even an extremely talented one with an extraordinary capacity for multitasking, is designed by God to do everything. Team ministry distributes the weight of serving. It allows people to do what they do best. It creates greater margin and focus and allows others to participate in what God is doing.

Jethro's counsel was right on target. He called for a

division of labor, some role clarity, and the appropriate stewardship of a team of leaders—not just one!

The Scriptures repeatedly indicate the importance of team. For example, when Paul addressed the diversity of spiritual gifts in Romans 12 and 1 Corinthians 12, he pointed out that while members of the body of Christ differ in their contribution, all are needed and must be employed for the proper functioning and unity of the church.

After spending time modeling and training the twelve disciples (a team of men), Jesus sent them out in pairs (a team) to do the work of ministry (Mark 6:7).

The New Testament frequently speaks of a team or group of elders giving oversight to the church in their city. And while difficult to fully comprehend, doesn't the Trinity—or one God consisting of three distinct persons, Father, Son and Holy Spirit—illustrate team? Each person is equal in His divine attribute but unique in function or role. All are equally omniscient, omnipotent, omnipresent, and unchanging. Yet to serve God's creation, humankind, all are needed, not just one.

Cohesive team relationships require mutual submission to God and to one another. This form of humility and surrender starts with a Spirit-led choice in the heart of each leader in favor of "team over me." Such submission is counter to culture. Instead of weakness, however, it creates great power.

Dr. Stephen R. Covey talks about this power in Primary Greatness: "Today's team leaders must look to new sources of power. The sources of their power are shifting: from position to persuasion, from charm to character, from control to service and sacrifice, from pride to humility, and from credentials to continuous learning and improvement."[27]

These kinds of power shifts, or inside-out transformations, are not something you read about and learn immediately. Rather, team power is learned over time with trial and error and a desire for improvement.

I marvel at all God taught me about myself and team leadership during my years at Fellowship Bible Church Little Rock. Bill Parkinson and Robert Lewis were great partners, both as elders and teaching pastors. We discovered that our different gifts and abilities were a wonderful complement to one another. We did not understand the concept of team at the beginning as well as we do now, but we started with a deeply held commitment to team. It was core to our leadership.

This conviction was clearly reflected in our approach to team teaching. Our shared pulpit relieved the constant pressure of weekly sermon preparation by a single person. Dividing this responsibility allowed more time for preparation, which enhanced the quality of our content and communication.

Different preaching styles and personalities helped us to connect better with more people in our congregation. In most instances, members never knew who was scheduled to deliver the message, but that didn't matter. Rather, it tended to add a sense of surprise and anticipation in our services.

Team permitted us to assign other leadership roles according to each man's design and unique abilities. The longer we served with one another, the better we understood the power and synergy of team.

Among the three of us, Robert was most gifted in providing vision for the church. Bill loved shepherding people and discipleship, which he is still doing at Fellowship. My roles tended to be more management-oriented and special project leadership. Of course, we all conducted weddings, funerals, baptisms, and Communion services.

Team also allowed us greater freedom and time to give ourselves to our families. It improved the overall quality of our lives, making us feel less stressed and more rested. In other words, team distributes pressure.

Team was also revealed in our collaborative decision-making process in our elders' meetings and staff strategizing sessions. We were committed to unanimity in all our decisions. This approach required more time and interaction than a majority vote would have demanded.

Nonetheless, we believed that our method protected our congregation and us from one-sided error. It also protected us from impulsivity and considering only a limited perspective on a matter. We learned to value the wisdom and counsel of shared leadership over our own opinions.

We believed in "team over me."

We were not perfect in this endeavor, nor did we become team experts. I'm merely communicating that we learned a lot over three decades together processing and integrating these ideals into our approach to leadership.

A case in point was an off-site planning day early in our relationship, when I discovered that I was one of the agenda items. Bill, Robert, and I were meeting at a friend's home where we could enjoy a quiet, private environment with no distractions. However, I was not aware of what was about to take place.

Our planning day began with Bill and Robert confronting me about making many important leadership decisions without their input. It wasn't that they distrusted me. It was more that they were feeling devalued by me. In their opinion, some adjustments needed to be made.

At first their surprise comments stung me. Like Moses,

I was starting to do too much on my own. During our discussion, however, I saw their point and apologized. Of course, they forgave me. God used my brothers to help me see a blind spot. They reminded me that there is greater wisdom in a team than there is in just one.

Because of this interaction, our mutual trust and respect for one another increased. We became more unified, and our team felt even stronger. I believe that we were able to resolve this issue quickly that day because we had a preexisting commitment to the value and advantages of team in our hearts.

Years later our elder board decided to capture some of what we had learned about the value of team that had served all of us so well. With the Lord's help, we determined to record them on a single sheet of paper so that they could be easily shared. As you might imagine, our single page was drafted, refined, rewritten, and reevaluated several times. We desired to put into words a simple definition of team and some of the benefits and challenges we had experienced.

I have included the document that resulted from our board interactions. In fact, I am still using it to train leaders about the virtues of team leadership.

Team Ministry is a collaborative philosophy of leadership embraced by leaders who are unified by a shared vision, function in roles according to their God-given design, and humbly submit to God and one another.

TEAM is:

Some Benefits

"...more organic than organizational in nature."

- Promotes a more wisdom based approached to decision-making
- Spreads out the pressure of ministry responsibilities
- Positions leaders according to their God-given strengths and abilities
- Values functional role clarity more than hierarchal position or status
- Fuels greater trust through mutual submission

"...a unique partnership recognizing complementary gifts and abilities."

Some Challenges

- Requires more time, greater patience and perseverance
- Demands a willingness to be personally vulnerable
- Chooses in favor of "team over me"
- Flexes with regard to role clarity as the church grows
- Exposes comparison, jealousy, competition, and control issues

"...having a team leader who catalyzes the team to accomplish the mission."

Application at Fellowship

- We will continue to strive for healthy TEAM MINISTRY at all levels of leadership, including elder, staff leadership, and lay teams.

"...when everyone on the team fully embraces and inspires others to pursue a shared vision."

- TEAM MINISTRY does not replace or supplant organizational governance, structure, authority, and oversight in staff functions.

- The Teaching Pastor Team is the most public statement of our commitment to TEAM MINISTRY.

God revealed to us that team embodies the spiritual passion a group of Christ followers has for working together to accomplish a greater result than can be achieved individually. As research analyst George Barna concludes, "Leadership works best when it is provided by teams of gifted leaders serving together in pursuit of a clear and compelling vision. . . . Team leadership is the only approach that carries the promise of satisfying the needs of our society. Solo leaders will always have an important place in our present and future reality, but teams hold the key to the future."[28]

Team leadership glorifies God, but it is hard work because it requires *heart* work to develop three essential characteristics:

- » patience in decision-making

- » a willingness to be vulnerable

- » relinquishing control

It all boils down to trust. Without trust, a marriage relationship will suffer. Without trust, a business partnership will break down. Without trust, church leadership teams will fail. Journalist H. L. Menchen once remarked, "For it is mutual trust, even more than mutual interest, that holds human associations together."[29]

When trust is lost, it tends to be replaced by a long list of team destroyers. Behaviors such as suspicion, comparison, competition, undermining, demonizing, and relational withdrawal tend to move in. Unaddressed, these behaviors wrongly begin to make us believe that we do not need one another, that team does not work, that it is too much trouble, or that we are better off alone.

These beliefs are simply not true. We are hard-wired by God for relationships. Together is always better than alone. When team is characterized by leaders who humbly submit to God and one another, even the restoration of lost trust is possible.

In *Managing the Non-Profit Organization* Drucker observes, "The leaders who work most effectively, it seems to me, never say 'I' and that's not because they have trained themselves not to say 'I.' They don't think 'I,' they think 'we'; they think 'team.' They understand their job to be to make team function. They accept responsibility and don't sidestep it, but 'we' gets the credit. .... This is what creates trust, what enables you to get the task done."[30]

Solomon, the wisest man to ever live, summed up team this way:

> Two are better than one because they have a good return for their labor. For if either of them falls, the one will lift up his companion. But woe to the one who falls when there is not another to lift him up. Furthermore, if two lie down together they keep warm, but how can one be warm alone? And if one can overpower him who is alone, two can resist him. A cord of three strands is not quickly torn apart. (Ecclesiastes 4:9–12 NASB)

Did you catch Solomon's conclusion? The combination of you, your partners, and the Lord of the universe are the "three strands" woven together that form team strength.

Another Leader's Story

by Brandon Washington

I grew up in a tradition that emphasized the value of a single omni-competent leader. I believed that good leaders had no weaknesses and were able to take a group of people on their proverbial backs and carry them on to victory.

This perspective deleteriously informed the manner in which I understood the practices of historical leaders. I imagined men like Martin Luther King Jr. and Vernon Grounds going into a private room and developing an ironclad vision on their own. I presumed they would emerge from their secluded space and assign to their teammates the roles they would play in the fulfillment of a polished vision. Their teammates were nothing more than wingmen who would serve at the pleasure of the leader in the fulfillment of his impeccable plan.

As it relates to leadership, this is all I knew. Moreover, such a perspective reconciled with my personality. I am a hyper-confident, opinionated, vocal, and large man. Such a cocktail of characteristics lends itself to a leadership model in which I am licensed to dictate the course of action, and everyone else is obliged to obey. This model was all I had ever known, and I wholeheartedly affirmed it.

In the fall of 2010 my wife and I relocated to Little Rock, Arkansas, where I initiated a residency at Fellowship Associates. We were there for training and mentoring in preparation for planting the Embassy Church in Denver, Colorado. I brought with me my perceptions regarding leadership. Consequently, my expectations of the residency fixated on the practical means by which my mentors would assist me in the execution of my plan.

Fellowship Associates had a better idea. While they did intend to help me refine and implement my vision for the church, they spent notably more time on me. To this day, their approach to my leadership development is the most shocking discipleship I have ever experienced. I was dazed by the manner in which they handled my weaknesses.

Under the dictates of my previous understanding of leadership, my assumption was that leaders seek to eliminate weaknesses. This was not the Fellowship Associates approach! For the first time in my life, mentors directed me to fixate on augmenting my strengths while surrounding myself with complementary teammates who are strong in my areas of weakness. Such an approach required a revised understanding of team. My cohorts are not wingmen; they are fellow leaders. In an effort to have the team function as a cohesive unit, I am compelled to submit to my teammates as they use their gifts toward the fulfilment of the mission that we share. Since I function as the team's primary vision caster, there are occasions when my voice is heard with greater weight, but there is never an occasion when my voice is imbued with greater authority.

As a team comprised of diverse strengths and personality types, we value mutual submission as essential to our well-being. Accordingly, I am not *the* sole leader; we lead as a team. Our decisions are made by consensus, and the entire team is willing to submit to the observations and concerns of one team member.

The idea of a team that values mutual submission has been met with resistance. Prior to planting the church, we sought funding to cover our operating cost. Without exception, every person and organization that chose to withhold their support cited our team model as a stumbling block. Repeatedly we were asked, "But who is *the guy* who will make final decisions?" They were applying the myth of the omni-competent leader. This occurred so often that, as a team, we agreed upon a united response. Our reply was "We believe the benefits of team far outweigh the complexities. All the obstacles are rendered moot if we model patient submission to gifted co-leaders. Such an approach allows for decisions that are superior to those of an individual."

The Embassy Church is now six years old. Our team model has resulted in healthier leaders and admirable decision-making. With conviction, we are able to say that we would choose no other model of leadership.

— BRANDON WASHINGTON is pastor of preaching and vision/elder at the Embassy Church in Denver, Colorado.

What About You?

〜

"Search me, God, and know my heart; test me and know my anxious thoughts. See if there is any offensive way in me, and lead me in the way everlasting."

— *Psalm 139:23–24 NIV*

Reflect

» Do you have a need to keep things under your control?

» Are you willing to function in a role consistent with your God-given design for the good of the leadership team and those they serve?

» Presently, would you describe yourself as feeling isolated and alone or relationally connected and a valued team member?

» Do you wholeheartedly believe that together is better than alone?

» With the Spirit's empowerment, what can you do to promote a culture of trust and honesty in your work environment?

Record

Write down your thoughts, feelings, action steps, questions, and anything else God reveals to your heart.

_____

_____

_____

_____

_____

_____

Remember:

- Team is a collaborative philosophy of
  leadership embraced by leaders who
  are unified by a shared vision, function
  according to their complementary gifts
  and abilities, and humbly submit to God
  and to one another.

- Team is fueled by the spiritual passion
  of a group of individuals to accomplish
  greater results together than could ever be
  achieved alone.

- Team leaders comprehend that vulnera-
  bility-based trust is the glue that builds
  great teams and glorifies God. They model this for others.

Chapter 5

VOLUNTARY SLAVERY

~

"True greatness, true leadership, is achieved not by
reducing men to one's service, but in giving
oneself in selfless service to them."
- J. Oswald Sanders

IT WAS AN ACTION-PACKED WEEK IN THE
life of Jesus. The celebration of Passover was near.
Jesus was leading His disciples on the road to Jerusalem.
For the third time He took the twelve aside to foreshadow
His upcoming death and resurrection.

He explained, "Behold, we are going up to Jerusalem
and the Son of Man will be delivered to the chief priests
and the scribes and they will condemn Him to death and
will deliver Him to the Gentiles. And they will mock

Him and spit upon Him, and scourge Him and kill Him, and three days later He will rise again" (Mark 10:33–34 NASB).

It is intriguing that this was the time Jesus chose to address two contrasting styles of leadership. One would think He would be distracted by the events before Him, but He was not. Perhaps the recent request from James and John for positions of status and the indignant feelings of the other disciples toward them influenced Jesus to describe genuine spiritual leadership at this time (Mark 10:35–41).

> And Jesus called them to him and said to them, "You know that those who are considered rulers of the Gentiles lord it over them, and their great ones exercise authority over them. But it shall not be so among you. But whoever would be great among you must be your servant, and whoever would be first among you must be slave of all. For even the Son of Man came not to be served but to serve, and to give his life as a ransom for many." (Mark 10:42–45)

Inside-out leadership is not about manipulation, coercion, status, or being in control of everything and everyone. It is not a "lord it over" dictatorial attitude but rather the attitude of a "slave of all." It has nothing to do with arrogance and everything to do with humility.

In his book *Spiritual Leadership* J. Oswald Sanders explains *inside-out* leadership this way: "The true leader will have no desire to lord it over God's heritage, but will be humble, gentle, self-sacrificing and altogether as ready to follow as to lead, when the Spirit makes it clear that a wiser and more gifted man than himself has appeared."[31]

In the phrase Jesus uses, "slave of all," the Greek word for *slave* is *doulos*, meaning "bondslave." The lives of voluntary slaves of Christ are unmistakably marked by three courageous choices:

- to be owned by Another

- to have no rights

- to accomplish the will of their Master

This is the case with Jesus. Notice Paul's description of Him as a bondslave:

> Do nothing from selfishness or empty conceit, but with humility of mind regard one another as more important than yourselves; do not merely look out for your own personal interests, but also for the interests of others.

> Have this attitude in yourselves which was also in Christ Jesus, who, although He existed in the form of God, did not regard equality with God a thing to be grasped, but emptied Himself, taking the form of a bond-servant, and being made in the likeness of men.

> Being found in appearance as a man, He humbled Himself by becoming obedient to the point of death, even death on a cross. (Philippians 2:3–8 NASB)

Jesus said of Himself, "My food is to do the will of Him who sent Me and to accomplish his work" (John 4:34). That's bondslave language. Bondslave leaders understand, like Jesus, that the way up is down.

Crawford Loritts, senior pastor of Fellowship Bible Church of Roswell, Georgia, explains, "I believe the key is embracing servant leadership not as a strategy but as an identity."[32]

Mike learned how to be a bondslave leader when he and his wife received a surprising calling to the mission field. It was not that he and his wife, Lyn, did not believe in missions; they just believed it was something others were called to do.

Then Mike's sixth-grade daughter, Kelly, announced that she wanted to become a full-time missionary. Thinking she would change her mind before becoming an adult, Mike did not take her too seriously. But Kelly continued to bring her desire to her parents' attention.

In eleventh grade Kelly asked if she could go on a mission trip with World Gospel Outreach (WGO) to Tegucigalpa, Honduras. Mike and Lyn agreed, believing some ground-level experience in a third-world country would soften her interest. Instead, she returned home more enthusiastic than ever!

That was when Mike decided that his family would go together the following year for a one-week ministry experience in Honduras. Mike and Lyn wanted to see the mission field and understand firsthand Kelly's passion, especially if they were to release their daughter to it.

Surprisingly, this trip and others that followed revealed to Mike and Lyn that the Lord was using their daughter to pursue them, not her, to become full-time missionaries in Honduras. Mike learned that WGO needed someone onsite to oversee and coordinate ministry operations. This was a perfect fit for him and an undeniable call from God on his life.

Lyn and Mike talked, prayed, and sought godly counsel to confirm this radical step of faith. They both reached the point in their journey at which they would have no peace without going.

The cost of saying yes to God's call on their lives was significant. At the time, Mike was enjoying a successful business partnership in construction. Lyn had a great job with a company she had been with for ten years. They loved their church. They would be moving away from parents, siblings, a daughter who was now in college, and many other meaningful friendships. Mike was concerned about how God would provide financially for his family in this new faith-based endeavor. They also needed language school training.

Mike and Lyn were leaving their culture and their comfort for an entirely new way of life. He said, "I was forty-four years old and left during my peak earning years, when we should have been paying off our home and contributing to a retirement plan." In spite of these challenges to life as he had known it, Mike said yes to God's call. He chose to become a voluntary slave of Christ. Mike has been serving in Honduras as the president and CEO for World Gospel Outreach for the last eighteen years.

This year alone nine hundred people will volunteer to join WGO on short-term mission trips to serve several thousand Honduran people who have no health care. Rancho Ebenezer, an orphanage built by WGO for abandoned children, provides loving care, proper nutrition, and a first-class education for them. "Pure and undefiled religion in the sight of our God and Father is this: to visit orphans and widows in their distress" (James 1:27 NASB).

"If given the opportunity, we would make the same choice again," Mike said. And Kelly? While continuing to support missions, she found Chris, a mate for life, in college. They got married and live in Austin, Texas, with their six children.

As we can see from Mike's life, bondslave leadership is not simply a role we choose to play but rather the kind of leader we aspire to become for the glory of God. Bondslaves possess an attitude of radical trust in Someone else no matter what He asks them to do.

One of the best examples of this attitude is Mary, a young girl, pregnant out of wedlock. In spite of facing public ridicule, shame, embarrassment to her family, and potentially being put away by her fiancé, she boldly said to the angel Gabriel, "Behold, the bondslave of the Lord; may it be done to me according to your word" (Luke 1:38 NASB). Facing unimaginable fear and uncertainty regarding her circumstances, Mary still chose to accomplish the will of her Master. What a great picture of *inside-out* leadership!

Conversely, following Jesus's arrest at Gethsemane, Peter denied even knowing Jesus on three occasions in the courtyard of the high priest. He became completely overwhelmed by a fear of being exposed as a disciple. His threatening circumstances on the outside were more powerful than the internal spiritual convictions of his heart. He did not respond from the *inside-out*.

The contrasting styles of leadership are illustrated below by two pyramids. One is drawn in the traditional, top-down fashion; the other is a non-traditional inverted pyramid. They are based on Jesus's words to His disciples and reveal His perspective.

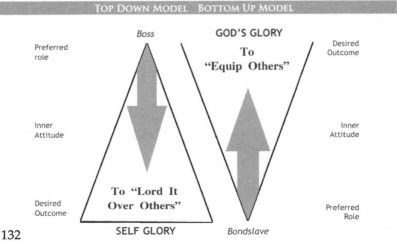

Note that it is not just the organizational structure but more importantly the inner attitude of the leader that is significant. In other words, not all top-down organizational structures have leaders with a "lord it over them" attitude, but most organizations in our world, both sacred and secular, are led this way.

In the top-down approach, status, power, and the number of people the leader has working under and for him or her are highly valued. Bosses with a dictatorial attitude position themselves at the apex of the pyramid. They are rulers of their empires.

In this organizational culture, people tend to feel micromanaged. Bosses must approve all decisions and must receive the adulation and applause for any success. This approach stifles individual creativity and ownership. It is a model that is primarily for the benefit of the insiders (the boss and a few elites), not for the outsiders—the customers, clients, congregation, or community.

In the model taught and exemplified by Jesus, leaders position themselves at the bottom of the inverted pyramid. They are still located at the apex, but the feel of the organizational culture is totally different.

Their role and passion are to set up others to win both inside and outside the borders of their church or company.In his book *Good to Great*, Jim Collins explains how these leaders "channel their ego needs from themselves and into the larger goal of building a great company. It's not that leaders have no ego or self-interest. Indeed, they are incredibly ambitious—but their ambition is first and foremost for the institution, not themselves."[33]

As was true of Jesus's leadership, arrogance is out, while humility is in. In opposition to a controlling, lording-it-over-them style of leadership, bondslave leaders equip and empower their employees to serve the needs of others, as Paul revealed: "And he gave the apostles, the prophets, the evangelists, the shepherds and teachers, to equip the saints for the work of ministry, for building up the body of Christ" (Ephesians 4:11–12).

Or as Peter exhorted leaders of the church, "Shepherd the flock of God that is among you, exercising oversight, not under compulsion, but willingly, as God would have you; not for shameful gain, but eagerly; not domineering over those in your charge, but being examples to the flock. And when the chief Shepherd appears, you will receive the unfading crown of glory" (1 Peter 5:2–4). The bondslave's overwhelming desire is for God to be glorified by the actions of everyone involved and in their successes.

The open-ended, bottom-up model exists for the benefit of the outsiders: customers, clients, congregation, and community. It is an atmosphere of low control and high accountability where the dignity and contribution of each person is recognized.

In his book *Drucker and Me* Bob Buford says that one of the great lessons he learned from his mentor, Peter Drucker, was "his conviction that an organization begins to die the day it begins to be run for the benefit of the insiders and not for the benefit of the customers."[34] In short, the "lording it over others" style of leadership, for the benefit of insiders, breeds death. The bondslave style of leadership, for the benefit of outsiders, is a life-giving adventure for everyone, and it glorifies God!

I wish I had understood more about being a voluntary slave, or *doulos*, for Christ when I began leading a church in 1977. I was twenty-eight years old and had what I refer to as "young man's disease." I recall being much more focused on my personal development than I was on becoming a "slave of all."

I was in a growing-up phase, wrestling with trying to figure out what I was good at doing and what I was not. I thought I had the right motives. I was working hard to be faithful and develop a good reputation. I wanted to cultivate the trust of others, and I had a desire to put my fingerprints on something meaningful. God used everything and wasted nothing to help me gradually learn that life is not about me; life is about Him. Still, I can't help but wonder what the kingdom impact might have been in my ministry if I had comprehended sooner the significance of becoming a bondslave for Christ.

How about you? Do you desire to become a voluntary slave for the glory of God? If so, how do you do it? The answer is—you cannot! You don't have the ability or the resources.

Even when aspiring to become bondslaves, leaders must fully comprehend and place their trust in the greatest act of bondslave leadership ever. Of course, I am referring to the life, death, and resurrection of Jesus Christ. His crucifixion and resurrection change everything!

The apostle Paul wrote about the impact of Jesus's sacrifice,

> For the love of Christ controls us, because we have concluded this: that one has died for all, therefore all have died; and he died for all, that those who live might no longer live for themselves but for him who for their sake died and was raised (2 Corinthians 5:14–15).

Paul makes it clear that before we can become bondslave leaders, we must place our trust in the radical grace of God toward us through His Son. He lived a sinless life and paid the penalty we owe for the sinful lives we are predisposed to live.

This same radical grace not only provides the resources for our new spiritual birth but also brings Christ's life into us by the Holy Spirit. The Spirit shapes us into a new kind of person or "a new creation" with transformed motivations (2 Corinthians 5:17). Not only have our hearts been changed but our purpose for living has changed as well. His radical grace changes us from the *inside-out*.

Then our aspiration to become a bondslave leader is not because we should or because it is the right thing to do. It is because of our growing love for God and all that Jesus has done for us. "For the love of Christ controls us," stated Paul (2 Corinthians 5:14). The Holy Spirit, our Advocate and Comforter, supplies the inner source of power and guidance we need to become increasingly conformed to the image of Jesus in every area of life for the glory of God.

In short, to aspire to become a bondslave we must experience a growing intimacy with the Bondslave. As Jesus explained, "Apart from me you can do nothing" (John 15:5).

Another Leader's Story

by Hunter Beaumont

When Bill asked for my reflections on "voluntary slavery," I knew he was actually asking for my musings on pain. If I've achieved any downward momentum, it's only through pain, none of which came voluntarily. Therefore, the correct title of my story is "Voluntary Slavery Learned Involuntarily Through Pain and Still Not Wholly Embraced by the Author."

My leadership story began when two friends and I set out to plant a church on the urban plains of Colorado. We had innocently adopted the noble ideas of the previous chapter, "Team over Me," and had voted me team leader, which felt great because I like to win elections. I had built a résumé of "little p" political skills such as explaining things, giving good speeches, telling jokes, dressing to impress, being nice to everyone's faces, and smoothing things over. It was easy to label this "leadership ability" or, even better, "servant leadership"! It would be years before a counselor helped me see that some of this is actually neurosis, the fear that someone somewhere is upset with me.

My first lesson came in the church's first year. We were struggling to grow our initial group of committed people to pursue the vision for launching the church we had cast. Despite our efforts, it felt as if something were missing. We were facing some difficult decisions that were going to be hard to explain, couldn't be glossed over with humor, would make some people unhappy, and required being honest to everyone's face. It felt as though our success were on the line. This was not the kind of leadership I had signed up for!

Ten of our core team eventually left. Friendships were strained. Motives were questioned. And I began an it's-going-to-take-the-rest-of-your-life struggle to learn the difference between servant leadership and keeping people happy.

Bill wisely writes, "*Inside-out* leadership is not about manipulation, coercion, status, or being in control of everything and everyone." But I did not realize that controlling everything and everyone can sometimes look like niceness and politeness as I rush to avoid a difficult conversation. Then he writes, "The lives of bondslaves of Christ are unmistakably marked by three courageous choices: to be owned by Another; to have no rights; to accomplish the will of their Master." But I did not understand that accomplishing the will of my Master can make others very uncomfortable, thus making me uncomfortable too.

Again and again Jesus has invited me out into uncertain waters. At each place of meaningful kingdom advancement, I've had to cross one or both of these barriers:

1. Where we need to go upsets the comfort of some.

2. The good of the team conflicts with the will of an individual.

Not long ago I lay on my sofa one Sunday afternoon distressed by people's distress, having just announced that we were several hundred thousand dollars short of where we needed to be in a building project. I could not differentiate the understandably anxious questions from the congregation from the voice of accusation in my head.

Then some other questions came with holy force: "Did I call you to this? Did I promise it would make everyone happy? Show me in My Word where it says, 'Follow me and I will make you fishers of compliments.'"

I meekly responded with orthodox answers, though my heart wasn't feeling them. Then the voice in my head changed. "I love you. I am with you." The Lord was reminding me that He will never leave or forsake me. He wants me to trust Him with everything, especially the way I lead others. Jesus's example of leadership was that of a voluntary slave. He accomplished the work His Father sent Him to do. With His help, I want to become more like Him.

— HUNTER BEAUMONT is lead pastor of Fellowship Denver in Denver, Colorado.

What About You?

~

"Search me, God, and know my heart; test me and know my anxious thoughts. See if there is any offensive way in me, and lead me in the way everlasting."

— *Psalm 139:23–24 NIV*

Reflect

» What motivates you the most—your personal achievements or how you might contribute to the needs of others?

» On a scale with arrogance on one end and humility on the other, where would you position yourself? Why there?

» Would you be willing to relinquish part of your leadership role to someone else who is clearly wiser and more gifted than you for the benefit of others?

» Is there a situation in your life where you need to say, "Not my will but Thy will be done"?

Record

Write down your thoughts, feelings, action steps, questions, and anything else God reveals to your heart.

_____

_____

_____

_____

_____

_____

Remember:

- Leaders recognize Jesus as the preeminent example of voluntary slavery to accomplish the will of Another.

- Bondslave leaders equip and empower those inside the organization in order to benefit those they serve outside the organization.

- Leaders choose to become voluntary slaves because of their growing love and affection for the Bondslave and their desire to glorify their Heavenly Father.

Chapter 6

ABIDING FRIENDSHIP

~

"What is my spiritual life? A love union with Jesus
in which the divine and the human
give themselves completely to one another."
— *Mother Teresa*

B ORN A PEASANT IN THE SEVENTEENTH
century in Lorraine, France, Nicolas Herman was
not a well educated man. After leaving the military with
chronic pain and a disability that would last for the rest
of his life, he took a job as a footman but discovered he
was clumsy and tended to break things. It is no wonder
he thought he did not amount to much and was not
good at anything. Eventually he found work in a French
monastery as a kitchen aide. In the later years of his life
his responsibilities shifted to repairing sandals.

Amazingly, this same man became one of history's most admired and well-known leaders because of his abiding friendship with God. Brother Lawrence, as Nicolas came to be called, loved the Lord dearly and delighted to be in His company. In the course of his repetitious chores, he determined to make his contributions an act of worship and praise. He cultivated a remarkable friendship with God by communing with Him during his work all day long.

"I worshiped Him as often as I could. I kept my mind in His holy presence. I recalled His presence as often as I found my mind wandering from Him. I found this to be a very difficult exercise! Yet I continued despite the difficulties I encountered. . . . Nonetheless, when we are faithful to keep ourselves in His holy presence and to set His face always before us, there is a good result."[35] He referred to this continual communion with God as the "practice of the presence of God."[36]

Shouldn't this abiding friendship that Brother Lawrence enjoyed with God be the longing of all Christ followers? It is seldom, however, that we hear men or women talk about their delight in "practicing the presence of God."

Brother Lawrence's character and unique friendship with Jesus attracted many leaders of his day to seek spiritual wisdom and guidance. Books written from his notes and teachings have blessed generations.

When I use the words "abiding friendship" or "delighting in God's company," I am not referring to pursuing more Bible study, attending conferences, or reading devotional literature. These are important and have a valuable place in the life of a Christ follower, but I am addressing the need for a leader to cultivate, with God's help, an open, authentic, ongoing, heart-level connection with the King of the universe. It is more about a growing, intimate, relational encounter with the Lord than it is learning more information about Him.

In his 1950 book *Divine Conquest* A. W. Tozer notes that most of us who call ourselves Christians do so on the basis of belief more than experience. He argues, "We have substituted theological ideas for an arresting encounter; we are full of religious notions, but our great weakness is that for our hearts there is no one there. . . . Knowledge by acquaintance," Tozer affirms, "is always better than mere knowledge by description."[37]

The Scriptures are clear that God both delights in us and desires for us to experience this abiding friendship. The psalmist captures God's delight when he says, "The Lord takes pleasure in those who fear him, in those who hope in his steadfast love" (Psalm 147:11).

The prophet Zephaniah proclaimed to Israel, "The LORD your God is in your midst, a mighty one who will save; he will rejoice over you with gladness; he will quiet you by his love; he will exult over you with loud singing" (Zephaniah 3:17).

Jesus's words to His disciples reveal His desire for intimate friendship:

> This is My commandment, that you love one another, just as I have loved you. Greater love has no one than this, that one lay down his life for his friends. You are My friends if you do what I command you. No longer do I call you slaves, for the slave does not know what his master is doing; but I have called you friends, for all things that I have heard from My Father, I have made known to you. You did not choose Me, but I chose you,

and appointed you that you should go and bear fruit, and that your fruit should remain, so that whatever you ask of the Father in My name He may give to you. This I command you, that you love one another. (John 15:12–17 NASB)

Sandwiched between the repeated commands to "love one another" as we have been loved by Jesus is His desire for intimacy with His disciples. In this text He includes three insights of an abiding friendship with Him.

The first insight, underlying all others, is that Jesus laid down His life for His friends. This includes you and me. In an act of extravagant love, He provided a pathway for an intimate, abiding friendship.

Jesus said, "I am the way, and the truth, and the life. No one comes to the Father except through me" (John 14:6). Then, three times in this passage He referred to us as His friends or His chosen ones.

The second insight is that Jesus desires to share privileged information with us that He has heard from His Father.

You might call this insider information, the kind close friends might share with one another.

The third insight Jesus communicated is that He has appointed us for a common purpose: to go and bear the fruit of an abiding friendship with Him for the glory of God. It is the privilege of being an "ambassador of Christ" in the world. The apostle Paul confirms this: "Therefore, we are ambassadors for Christ, as though God were making an appeal through us; we beg you on behalf of Christ, be reconciled to God" (2 Corinthians 5:20 NASB).

Also in John 15 Jesus spoke to His friends about what is essential to bearing this fruit:

> Abide in me, and I in you. As the branch cannot bear fruit by itself, unless it abides in the vine, neither can you, unless you abide in me. I am the vine; you are the branches. Whoever abides in me and I in him, he it is that bears much fruit, for apart from me you can do nothing. (John 15:4–5)

The fruit-bearing friendship Jesus desires with us is a close, dependent, intimate one. It is eternal in nature, involving the three persons of the Trinity and the powerful resources of each. It is an unearned, undeserved gift of grace!

Commenting on this, Mother Teresa writes, "What is my spiritual life? A love union with Jesus in which the divine and the human give themselves completely to one another."[38]

In light of this great passion on God's part for personal friendship, why is it that so few leaders are described as being friends with God? Abraham is the only person in the Old Testament who is specifically called "a friend of God" (2 Chronicles 20:7; Isaiah 41:8; James 2:23).

Why aren't more leaders delighted to invest time and energy to cultivate an abiding relationship with Christ? What stands in the way? Why do other things grab our greatest attention?

Looking back on my own spiritual journey, I'm shocked to see how easy it has been to pursue task accomplishment, other relationships, and new learning opportunities about God as substitutes for personal encounters with Him.

It has taken me a long time to begin connecting with Jesus at a heart level instead of just a head level. I have believed that God loves me. I have understood that I have been forgiven. I have acknowledged that the Holy Spirit lives within me, but I have been slow to be intimate and vulnerable with my Friend. I have realized that He will never leave me or forsake me, but I have missed out on being present to Him in my daily life, as did Brother Lawrence. I was lacking in my delight in His company and failing to love Him back for His delight in me. How offensive this must be to Jesus! Yet He still loves me and waits patiently for me to draw near to Him.

In recent years, thankfully, I have begun to experience more of the "love union" Mother Teresa described. I am encouraged and expectant about what God is doing in my heart today, but I feel there is much more for me to appreciate about giving myself completely to Jesus in friendship.

Tim Keller's book *The Prodigal God* is a must read. Using the familiar parable found in Luke 15, he insightfully pinpoints one of the major obstacles keeping us from an abiding friendship with God. Keller says that it is easy for us to see the disconnect in the heart of the younger son for his father. After all, he left home and squandered his inheritance in loose living. However, by the conclusion of the story, we discover that really both sons are rebellious and distant from their father's love and friendship.

Keller explains, "What did the older son most want? If we think about it we realize that he wanted the same thing as his brother. He was just as resentful of the father as was the younger son. He too wanted the father's goods rather than the father himself. . . . The hearts of the two brothers were the same."[39]

Even though the older brother had stayed home, worked hard, and obeyed his father's commands, his heart was not in touch with the heart of his father. He was physically near to his father, but he was not relationally close to him.

Is that it? As leaders, are we knowingly or unknowingly desiring the benefits of our Heavenly Father but not the Father Himself?

Are we celebrating our new birth, claiming God's promises, benefitting from His wisdom and perspective about life, and counting on a future hope in heaven but not really enjoying Him? Like the older brother, are we close to Him yet distant from Him at the same time?

I must confess that I can see myself in the life of the older brother. In a sense, I stayed home. I worked hard to follow God's commands. I was dutiful and responsible in my church leadership. I loved and led my wife and children the best I could. I tried to do the right thing, but sadly I wasn't really delighting in Him and didn't know how to do so.

In his *Maxims* Brother Lawrence explains, "Men invent means and methods of coming at God's love, they learn rules and set up devices to remind them of that love, and it seems like a world of trouble to bring oneself into the consciousness of God's presence. Yet it might be so simple. Is it not quicker and easier just to do our common business wholly for the love of Him?"[40]

The Old Testament reveals to us that David had a heart for God. He was not a perfect leader, but he spent many years of his life in the presence of the Lord. This is his wise counsel to us: "Delight yourself in the LORD, and he will give you the desires of your heart" (Psalm 37:4).

The word *delight* means to bend toward or incline toward. David was urging us to lean into God. He was pressing us to pursue companionship, abiding friendship, and a joyful preoccupation with the One who has transformed our lives forever. Simply put, we are being charged to find our greatest enjoyment in God alone.

Did you notice that delighting in the Lord precedes receiving the desires of our hearts? This strikes me as similar to the lesson learned from *The Prodigal God*. Find your enjoyment in the Father, not only in the Father's goods!

An *inside-out* leader comprehends that true self-fulfillment does not lie in a preoccupation with selfish desires but in a selfless preoccupation with God Himself.

Bill, the owner of Smith Capital Investment, had to learn how to switch his focus from himself to God. "Outwardly I had it all, but inwardly I was coming apart," he said. "I was religious in the sense that I worshiped many gods over the years. Success, hard work, money, position, power, and the high life were my gods. They all failed to deliver where it counted, in my heart."

Bill was searching for greater meaning and purpose in his life. Feeling the void, he pursued the beliefs and philosophies of several religions: Buddhism, Taoism, Zen, Hinduism, and many New Age derivations. None of these filled the void in his heart.

However, with some time to kill in a Salt Lake City hotel in June 1987, Bill opened the drawer of the bedside table and picked up a Gideon-placed Bible. He turned to the Gospel of John and began reading:

> In the beginning was the Word, and the Word was
> with God, and the Word was God. He was in the
> beginning with God. All things came into being by
> Him, and apart from Him nothing came into being
> that has come into being. In Him was life, and the

life was the Light of men. . . . He came to His own,
and those who were His own did not receive Him.
But as many as received Him, to them He gave the
right to become children of God, even to those who
believe in His name. (John 1:1–4, 11–12 NASB)

"For the first time I felt a surprising desire to respond
and move toward Him," said Bill. When he returned to
his home in Little Rock, he was determined to purchase
a Bible. In August 1987 he bought a copy of the *One-Year
Bible* and began his quest of friendship with Jesus Christ.

As Bill followed Jesus and His disciples through the
four Gospel accounts in his morning readings, he began
to sense God's presence. Jesus wanted an abiding
friendship with Bill, and Bill found Jesus irresistible.
Bill's greatest joy and purpose from this point until the
end of his earthly life became to know Him and make
Him known. This is exactly what he did.

Bill joined his pastor and friend Robert Lewis, the
founder of Men's Fraternity, to host and oversee early-
morning meetings about manhood to more than one

thousand men! He did this for the next ten years. What an opportunity to make Him known to other men!

The larger this ministry grew, the more time Bill gave by cutting back on his work schedule until he finally sold his company. This allowed Bill to meet regularly with men of all ages at his office to tell them how he had learned to spend time with Jesus.

Bill even wrote a booklet called *Quiet Time* from his experience of abiding with Him. He explains, "Quiet time is simply a daily experience with Jesus Christ from which our whole life draws direction, strength, joy, and vitality."[41]

As Charles Haddon Spurgeon said, "Those who delight in God desire or ask nothing but what will please God."[42] Yet we have His assurance that He will "supply every need of [ours] according to his riches in glory in Christ Jesus" (Philippians 4:19).

Practically speaking, how can you and I delight in God? How can a person pursue this abiding friendship or divine preoccupation?

Once again, we cannot do this by ourselves. We must rely upon the resources of God to encounter the person of God. The Holy Spirit has been given to come alongside us to supply the power for this aspect of our spiritual journeys. But we do need to humbly admit our inadequacies and yield to the Spirit's guidance and control.

There is not a formula or a one-size-fits-all process. As Brother Lawrence's abiding friendship with the Lord was unique, so will ours be special. Meaningful friendships are this way. They are unique to those involved.

Recently a church planter asked me, "What are you praying about personally these days?" I had a ready answer because God has been speaking to my heart about this for some time. I am praying about three areas to deepen my friendship with Christ.

First, I am asking the Holy Spirit to guide and empower me to become more alert and fully present to God throughout my daily life.

Dr. David Benner describes being present as "spiritual

attentiveness. . . . It is releasing distractions, preoccupations, and prejudgments and being available for absorption."[43]

Martha's sister Mary, seated at the feet of Jesus, was fully present to Him. Nothing was distracting her from deepening her friendship with Jesus.

Often I become aware that I am present to someone physically but my mind is preoccupied with something else. In other words, I am not all there. I also find that this often describes my relationship with God.

Because I desire to deepen my friendship with Him, I am becoming more vulnerable, honest, and conversational with Jesus about an issue I am facing, an unresolved conflict, or anything else that makes me feel troubled or stressed. Frequently this includes admitting my inability to clearly understand how I feel about something. I am asking Jesus to help me identify my emotions. I am also asking my Friend to reveal what He desires for me to learn about a circumstance rather than focusing on what others need to learn.

Simply put, I am praying regularly that the Spirit will make me more present to the Lord and His work in and through me. The Lord already knows everything about me before I do. So I am pursuing an ongoing daily dialogue with Him. It's one way I am delighting or leaning into my friendship with Jesus.

Second, I am praying that I will rely on the Spirit's power to love others the way that I have been loved by God. John reminds us of this love:

> Beloved, let us love one another, for love is from God, and whoever loves has been born of God and knows God. Anyone who does not love does not know God, because God is love. In this the love of God was made manifest among us, that God sent his only Son into the world, so that we might live through him. In this is love, not that we have loved God but that he loved us and sent his Son to be the propitiation for our sins. Beloved, if God so loved us, we also ought to love one another. (1 John 4:7–11)

These are powerful words. As I read them I realize I owe

a debt to my Savior to love others. He loved me before I even thought about loving Him.

I am depending on the Spirit to help me love others by giving them my full attention. I am seeking to listen to them without distraction and without interrupting them. I want to love others by being more fully present not only to the Lord but also to them.

This may sound simple, but we all know it is no small task to love others. On our own it is impossible, but we are not on our own.

Because God is love, because He has given me His presence in the person of the Holy Spirit to live in me, and because one of the fruits of the Spirit is love, then my abiding friendship with Jesus has provided all the resources I need to love others. With God's help I can learn to love others as I have been loved. Such love reflects that I am a friend of God.

Third, I am praying that I can deepen my abiding friendship by avoiding hurriedness.

"Be still, and know that I am God" (Psalm 46:10). This has become a growing desire and focus of mine over the last several years. While worldly culture values multitasking, climbing the ladder at all costs, and achieving the driven leader lifestyle, I do not.

I have experienced my own hurriedness as a great distraction and even an enemy to the abiding friendship with God that I desire to deepen. It is easy for leaders to get so busy that they have no time for friendship with God. It is easy to become a driven leader instead of a Spirit-led, *inside-out* leader.

In *Making All Things New* Henri Nouwen explains, "Without solitude it is virtually impossible to live a spiritual life. . . . We need to set aside a time and space to give him our undivided attention. Jesus says, 'Go to your private room and, when you have shut your door, pray to your Father who is in that secret place' (Matthew 6:6)."[44] Anything that distracts me from having a divine preoccupation is not good for my soul.

The Ephesian church was warned about this very issue:

I know your works, your toil and your patient endurance, and how you cannot bear with those who are evil, but have tested those who call themselves apostles and are not, and found them to be false. I know you are enduring patiently and bearing up for my name's sake, and you have not grown weary. But I have this against you, that you have abandoned the love you had at first. (Revelation 2:2–4)

Be careful when you are busy doing too much; it is easy to neglect or even forget your first love.

Like any other friendship, an abiding friendship with God is not an overnight process but a relational journey. It will have its ups and downs. You cannot instantly overcome all the things that distract you—the idols in your heart or anything that is crowding God out— but you can be certain of this: your Friend is waiting patiently, and He delights in your efforts.

Another Leader's Story

by Dave Furman

I came to the Middle East to change the world, but instead God changed me.

I was excited to start a new church planting work in the fastest- growing city in the world. I had been through various trainings and was ready to apply everything I knew to planting a new church. And then, in a moment, my world came crashing down.

About a month after we moved to the region, my health failed. We thought I had been healed from a debilitating nerve disease after previous surgeries, but the pain came back with a vengeance and was far worse than ever before. I was disabled and depressed.

There I was, ready to charge the hill for Jesus, and I couldn't even get off the couch. The days were long, but the nights were even longer. When the darkness would not lift I would pace up and down my bedroom floor yelling to and at God. The boils on my fingertips were excruciating and the burning pain in my elbows infuriating.

I couldn't do much of anything on my own. I was dependent on my wife to open doors for me, cook, put on my seatbelt, turn on the faucet, brush my teeth, and help me get dressed. The plans I had for my life were but shattered dreams. It felt as if God had brought me to the desert to destroy me.

But God had other plans. He wasn't hurting me; He was showing me that I needed an abiding friendship with Him.

It's not natural for me to sit, reflect, or stop. I am always on the go for what feels like twenty-four hours a day. I was running too fast—so fast that I was leaving Jesus behind. This is why Bill's chapter on abiding friendship is so important to me. I was reading my Bible and praying, but it was more of an item to check off on a long list. I wasn't delighting in God's company. As Bill says, I wasn't "having an open, authentic, on-going, heart-level connection with the King of the universe."

I needed to learn the message of Psalm 37:4—"Delight yourself in the LORD, and He will give you the desires of your heart."

My story doesn't have a happy ending the way most fairytales do. I'm not healed physically; I still struggle with chronic pain every hour of every day. There are still moments I'm tempted toward depression, and the nights are often long. But while I have yet to change the world, God certainly has changed me. I needed an abiding friendship with the King of kings. God stopped me in my tracks, broke me, and brought me into a deeper relationship with Him.

In spite of my prolonged journey with pain, God's abiding friendship has empowered me to experience ministry for Him beyond my greatest expectations.

I pray that in the days to come I will continue to grow in my friendship with God. That's my prayer for you too. Those of us who lead in God's kingdom should always be asking the Holy Spirit to guide and empower us to be more present to God throughout our days. The truth of this chapter is the key to leading well in God's kingdom. Our only hope is that we would not be so hurried in our work for God that we forget to spend time with God. May an abiding friendship with God be at the heart of all we do.

— *DAVE FURMAN is lead pastor of*
Redeemer Church of Dubai, United Arab Emirates.

What About You?

"Search me, God, and know my heart; test me and know my anxious thoughts. See if there is any offensive way in me, and lead me in the way everlasting."

— *Psalm 139:23–24 NIV*

Reflect:

» Do you allow task accomplishment to stand in your way of spending undisturbed time with Jesus?

» What distractions are you facing presently that are undercutting an abiding friendship with Him?

» Do you desire the benefits of your Heavenly Father but not the Father Himself?

» Is the pace of your life hurting or helping your friendship with God?

» How could you deepen this friendship at a heart level instead of just a head level?

169

Record

Write down your thoughts, feelings, action steps, questions, and anything else God reveals to your heart.

_____

_____

_____

_____

_____

_____

Remember:

- Leaders understand that their abiding friendship or union with Jesus Christ is absolutely essential for being an Ambassador for Christ in the world.

- Leaders are diligent to identify and avoid the things that distract them from the presence and power of God.

- Leaders rely completely on the powerful resources of the Trinity to protect and cultivate their delight in an abiding friendship with Jesus.

Chapter 7

HUMILITY

~

"Clothe yourselves with humility toward one another, for God is
opposed to the proud, but gives grace to the humble."
— *The Apostle Peter (1 Peter 5:5 NASB)*

H AVE YOU EVER NOTICED HOW A
season of success brings out arrogance in one
leader and humility in another?

Solomon, the wisest man to ever live, revealed these
contrasting outcomes:

> When pride comes, then comes dishonor, But with
> the humble is wisdom. (Proverbs 11:2 NASB)

Pride goes before destruction, And a haughty spirit before stumbling. It is better to be humble in spirit with the lowly Than to divide the spoil with the proud. (Proverbs 16:18–19 NASB)

James, the half-brother of Jesus, made it clear how the Lord feels about the issue: "God is opposed to the proud, but gives grace to the humble" (James 4:6 NASB).

John Dickson describes twentieth-century British writer G. K. Chesterton's belief about pride: "Human pride is in fact the engine of mediocrity. It fools us into believing that we have 'arrived,' that we are complete, that there is little else to learn."[45]

Our Heavenly Father's disdain for the arrogant, boastful, self-sufficient leader is obvious. Yet He promises wisdom and grace to the person with a humble spirit who trusts Him with everything.

In Judges 7 God called a prophet, judge, and military man named Gideon to lead a battle against the powerful army of the Midianites and the Amalekites.

Gideon's army was grossly outnumbered, and he seemed to be controlled by fear and doubt. He reacted to God's calling by requesting a sign that would prove he would be victorious:

> Then Gideon said to God, "If you will save Israel by my hand, as you have said, behold, I am laying a fleece of wool on the threshing floor. If there is dew on the fleece alone, and it is dry on all the ground, then I shall know that you will save Israel by my hand, as you have said." (Judges 6:36–37)

God answered his request to the letter, but that was not enough to arrest Gideon's fears. So he reversed his request: this time make the fleece dry and the ground around it wet. And God did that too.

But watch what took place next:

> Then Jerubbaal (that is, Gideon) and all the people who were with him rose early and camped beside the spring of Harod. And the camp of Midian was north of them, by the hill of Moreh, in the valley.

The LORD said to Gideon, "The people with you are too many for me to give Midianites into their hand, lest Israel boast over me, saying, 'My own hand has saved me.' Now therefore proclaim in the ears of the people, saying, 'Whoever is fearful and trembling, let him return home and hurry away from Mount Gilead.'" Then 22,000 of the people returned, and 10,000 remained.

And the LORD said to Gideon, "The people are still too many. Take them down to the water, and I will test them for you there, and anyone of whom I say to you, 'This one shall go with you,' shall go with you, and anyone of whom I say to you, 'This one shall not go with you,' shall not go." So he brought the people down to the water. And the LORD said to Gideon, "Every one who laps the water with his tongue, as a dog laps, you shall set by himself. Likewise, every one who kneels down to drink." And the number of those who lapped, putting their hands to their mouths, was 300 men, but all the rest of the people knelt down to drink water. And the LORD said to Gideon, "With the 300 men who lapped I will save you and give the

> Midianites into your hand, and let all the others go
> every man to his home." (Judges 7:1–7)

Can you imagine what Gideon must have been feeling? He was overwhelmingly outnumbered from the beginning. In fact, Judges 8:10 tells us that the size of the enemy army was about 135,000 men! Even with 32,000 men, the outlook appeared bleak.

Yet the Lord reduced the size of Gideon's forces twice. First God said "whoever is afraid and trembling" could go home. With God's permission, 22,000 left.

Then the Lord said, "The people are still too many." He required a drinking test this time, and only three hundred lappers were allowed to remain.

Can't you just see the fear and doubt overtaking Gideon's heart? But God assured him that He would deliver the Israelites. And He did so, amazingly, with the three hundred men carrying torches in clay jars and blowing trumpets.

Why did God require all the reductions of Gideon's army? The second verse of chapter 7 reveals the answer:

"The Lᴏʀᴅ said to Gideon, 'The people who are with you are too many for me to give the Midianites into their hand, lest Israel boast over me, saying, "My own hand has saved me."'"

God is establishing the distinction between a proud response to success and a humble response to success. It's not my own hand that has saved me, but the power of God has delivered me just as He promised.

Pride and boasting never glorify God. Humbly trusting Him with everything—even what seems to be a ridiculous battle plan with impossible odds for victory— always does.

Simply stated, "less of us and more of God" is always a winning leadership combination.

On many occasions in my life, pride surfaced during a successful endeavor. In some instances I wanted to be sure that everyone knew it was my idea that led to such a great outcome. At other times receiving the appropriate level of credit for my contribution was overly important to me. Even worse are the times when I have allowed people to believe I was the primary reason for a success when I was not. In other words, I was stealing credit for someone else's leadership.

Such selfish actions are encouraged and even rewarded by the world system. Climbing the corporate ladder, receiving bonuses, and gaining the favor of one's superiors seem to rest heavily on promoting personal accomplishments.

In contrast, author David Brooks writes, "You have to surrender to something outside yourself to gain strength within yourself. You have to conquer your desire to get what you crave. Success leads to the greatest failure, which is pride. Failure leads to the greatest success, which is humility and learning. In order to fulfill yourself, you have to forget yourself. In order to find yourself, you have to lose yourself."[46]

History records some incredible stories of success that demonstrate remarkable humility and a concern for the welfare of others. Consider Sir Edmund Hillary.

He was born on July 20, 1919, in Auckland, New Zealand.

As a youngster he was small, shy, and rather lonely. However, as a teenager, he grew to six feet, five inches, and discovered an unquenchable passion for mountain climbing.

In 1953 he was chosen to join the ninth expedition to Everest led by British Army Colonel John Hunt. On this expedition Hillary and his Sherpa guide, Tenzing Norgay, became the first two men to climb the 29,029-foot peak of Mount Everest. After this incredible accomplishment his fame was immediate. Never being interested in profiting himself, Hillary established the Himalayan Trust to build schools, airfields, and hospitals for the people of Nepal.

To quote John Dickson, "He epitomized the noble choice to forgo status, deploy resources, and use influence for the good of others before himself."[47]

The apostle Paul confirmed this description of humility: "Do nothing from selfishness or empty conceit, but with humility of mind regard one another as more important than yourselves; do not merely look out for your own personal interests, but also for the interests of others" (Philippians 2:3–4 NASB).

Mark Strom, historian and leadership analyst, offers this worldview:

"Wise leaders hold nobility with humility. Overbearing ego and debilitating self-abasement are generally avoided in all wisdom traditions. Many traditions call for balance. I would suggest a further step, also found in the ancient wisdom writings: that you look beyond balance, that you embrace the paradox of strength in weakness to find your true weight as a leader."[48]

What is "strength in weakness"? It is what Jesus modeled for His disciples in the Upper Room when He met with them to celebrate Passover.

Before we take a closer look at what He did, it is important to understand what He already knew as their leader.

First, "Jesus knew that His hour had come" (John 13:1).

It was time for Him to finish the work His Father had given Him. God would be glorified through Jesus's unjust execution and death. "Being found in appearance as a man, He humbled Himself by becoming obedient to the point of death, even death on a cross" (Philippians 2:8 NASB).

Second, Jesus knew that Judas would betray Him.

Jesus was aware of Satan's temptation of Judas, knowing that "the devil [had] already put into the heart of Judas Iscariot, the son of Simon, to betray Him" (John 13:2 NASB).

Third, Jesus knew His destiny.

He was aware that His physical presence on earth was coming to an end. Jesus was leaving those He loved. "Jesus [knew] that the Father had given all things into His hands, and that He had come forth from God and was going back to God" (John 13:3 NASB).

With a total awareness of these truths, what did Jesus do to leave a lasting impression on His leadership team?

> [He] got up from supper, and laid aside His garments; and taking a towel, He girded Himself. Then He poured water into the basin, and began

to wash the disciples' feet and to wipe them with the towel with which He was girded. So He came to Simon Peter. He said to Him, "Lord, do You wash my feet?" Jesus answered and said to him, "What I do you do not realize now, but you will understand hereafter." Peter said to Him, "Never shall you wash my feet!" Jesus answered him, "If I do not wash you, you have no part with Me." Simon Peter said to Him, "Lord, then wash not only my feet, but also my hands and my head." Jesus said to him, "He who has bathed needs only to wash his feet, but is completely clean; and you are clean, but not all of you." For He knew the one who was betraying Him; for this reason He said, "Not all of you are clean." So when he had washed their feet, and taken His garments and reclined at table again, He said to them, "Do you know what I have done to you? You call Me Teacher and Lord; and you are right, for so I am. If I then, the Lord and the Teacher, washed your feet, you also ought to wash one another's feet. For I gave you an example that you also should do as I did to you." (John 13:4–15 NASB)

Jesus gave His disciples and us a truly unforgettable lesson on the power of humility in leadership. The Master Teacher, the Sovereign, the Creator, the greatest Leader ever took on the role of a household slave to wash the feet of His guests. He voluntarily stooped to clean the dusty, dirty feet of others. And He made certain His disciples understood that they should follow His example. Jesus modeled an *inside-out* approach to leadership that was impossible to forget.

What was it like when He knelt before Judas? Did they make eye contact? What was Judas feeling? What was Jesus feeling as He held the feet of the traitor in His hands? What an incredible moment this must have been! Jesus was holding back on His power and what He knew about Judas in order to serve him. This is the power of authentic humility. There is no better example of strength in weakness.

It makes me wonder what level of conviction the disciples, who had just been arguing over who was the greatest among them, experienced as Jesus washed their feet. Perhaps they were beginning to comprehend that true greatness is found in service to others and not in personal status. Maybe it was starting to sink in that pride is the enemy of an *inside-out* leader and that God exalts humility.

Years later Peter wrote, "And all of you, clothe yourselves with humility toward one another, for God is opposed to the proud, but gives grace to the humble. Therefore humble yourselves under the mighty hand of God, that He may exalt you at the proper time" (1 Peter 5:5–6 NASB). You can almost be certain that this profound lesson on humility from the evening in the Upper Room crossed his mind when he wrote these verses.

Mother Teresa explained, "Humility is the mother of all virtues; purity, charity and obedience. It is in being humble that our love becomes real, devoted and ardent. If you are humble nothing will touch you, neither praise nor disgrace, because you know what you are. If you are blamed you will not be discouraged. If they call you a saint you will not put yourself on a pedestal."[49]

At one point Mother Teresa offered these fifteen guidelines to cultivating humility:

1. Speak as little as possible about yourself.

2. Keep busy with your own affairs and not those of others.

3. Avoid curiosity.

4. Do not interfere in the affairs of others.

5. Accept small irritations with good humor.

6. Do not dwell on the faults of others.

7. Accept censures even if unmerited.

8. Give in to the will of others.

9. Accept insults and injuries.

10. Accept contempt, being forgotten and disregarded.

11. Be courteous and delicate even when provoked by someone.

12. Do not seek to be admired and loved.

13. Do not protect yourself behind your own dignity.

14. Give in, in discussions, even when you are right.

15. Choose always the more difficult task.[50]

When the apostle Paul described the humility of Jesus, he used a profound two-word phrase: Jesus "emptied Himself" (Philippians 2:7 NASB). What does this unusual phrase mean?

One of the truths these words imply is that Jesus chose to hold back on His personal power for the eternal welfare of others and for the glory of His Father in heaven.

He held back from reacting to the insults of His enemies. He held back from trying to prove that they were wrong and He was right. He held back from attempting to control the situation. Even though He had the power to demonstrate His greatness, He did not.

I imagine that His silence appeared to His accusers to be a sign of weakness and passivity. Strangely, however, Jesus's humble act of emptying Himself revealed His freedom to trust His Father with everything. It is this freedom that resulted in the most powerful act of leadership the world has ever known!

Like Jesus, *inside–out* leaders pursue trusting God with everything. They realize that holding back from making a retaliatory statement defuses an unnecessary conflict. They understand that holding back from saying, "I told you so," allows a person to learn from failure without humiliation. They know that holding back from fighting for control means they no longer have anything to prove.

Such self-emptying choices may appear to a leader's adversaries as a sign of weakness or passivity, but in reality these decisions reflect a powerful inner freedom to lead for the welfare of others and for the glory of God.

According to Jim Collins, great leaders understand the difference between a window and a mirror. He states, "Level 5 leaders look out the window to apportion credit to factors outside themselves when things go well (and if they cannot find a specific person or event to give credit to, they credit good luck). At the same time they look in the mirror to apportion responsibility, never blaming bad luck when things go poorly."[51] He concludes, "Level 5 leaders embody a paradoxical mix of personal humility and professional will."[52]

It should be no surprise that I believe humility is the premier virtue of *inside-out* leadership. It is the spiritual thread that runs through the heart of all the other *inside-out* leadership virtues that are the subjects of this book. Humility empowers each one for greater impact in the leader's life and in the lives of those he or she serves.

As Stephen Covey states, "Humility truly is the mother of all virtues. It makes us a vessel, a vehicle, an agent instead of 'the source' or the principal. It unleashes all other learning, all growth and process."[53]

I have learned from God that humility is

- finding sufficiency in Christ, not self

- recognizing arrogance as an enemy of God

- having a nothing-to-prove attitude

- trusting God with everything

- listening intently to understand someone

- asking for forgiveness

- admitting that someone else is right and you are wrong

- responding to an insult with a blessing

- being willing to be vulnerable

- submitting voluntarily to the leadership of another

- choosing to embrace an unwanted reality

- providing for the welfare of others without a need for recognition

- waiting on the Lord

- confessing sin

Humility unleashes all other leadership virtues for greater impact. It is a divine gift that originates inside a leader and flows outwardly. Humility is the spiritual conviction that less of us and more of God is the winning combination of leadership for every circumstance in life.

Mere knowledge of this truth is not enough. Leaders cannot will themselves to be humble. It is not something to be achieved or earned; it is a *gift of grace*. Humility is a sacred trust that has been designed by the Father, modeled by the Son, and empowered by the Holy Spirit for those who are disciples of Christ. Louie Giglio, founder of the Passion Movement, observes, "Humility makes great leaders. Humility, by the way, is not a character trait we develop but a by-product of being with Jesus."[54]

Therefore, humility is forged over time in the context of a leader's complete surrender to the will and the way of Someone greater—Jesus Christ. This is not a quick process. It is a deliberate journey requiring ongoing, intimate encounters with the Father, Son, and Holy Spirit. Humility is obtained by leaders whose single focus in life is to live for the glory of God.

David Brooks describes the difference between résumé virtues and eulogy virtues in his introductory remarks in *The Road to Character*. Résumé virtues refer to a leader's vocational skills and abilities that contribute to his or her success. They are external in nature. Eulogy virtues refer to the ones that reveal the character of a leader's soul. They are internal in nature. These are the virtues that determine the kind of man or woman a person becomes. "They are the virtues that get talked about at your funeral," says Brooks.[55]

Résumé leaders are preoccupied with what they

can accomplish and attain. Eulogy leaders are more concerned with cultivating certain moral attributes and what they can contribute. Résumé leaders build a résumé to impress. Eulogy leaders build loving relationships and sacrifice themselves to benefit others. Résumé leaders live out of their heads. Eulogy leaders live from their hearts. All leaders must deal with the tension being expressed by these two approaches. The two need to be integrated for a leader to become whole.

Inside-out leaders are guided by their internal moral code to give perspective and empower their accomplishments in the world.

The seven leadership values in this book are eulogy virtues. I am convinced that the manner in which a leader pursues and incarnates them will determine the legacy of his or her life.

Another Leader's Story

by Jeremy Linneman

My journey as a leader has demanded an inward journey into my own loss, pain, and defenses. By facing God and my own story with honesty and vulnerability, I have found a path to what Bill calls "being rather than doing—an integration of one's head and one's heart."

My childhood was defined by several traumatic losses. My youngest sister, Amy, died shortly after birth when I was six years old. As a result of Amy's unexpected death, an environment of grief and loss permeated our home and my childhood. But when I was sixteen, tragedy struck again: My older brother, Joe, eighteen at the time, was killed suddenly in a car accident.

Losing Joe broke my heart. I'll never forget the doctor's exact words to my family in that beige consultation room. I'll never forget running away to find an empty place in the hospital to collapse in shock, grief, and anger. But I'll also never forget how the Lord met me in that moment—joining me in my pain, speaking softly to me, and drawing me to Himself.

Unfortunately, I continued to live with the loss. I struggled for years with insomnia, depression, and later chronic pain and fatigue. As I tried to move on from grief and pain, my body kept score. I entered pastoral ministry in my early twenties hoping to encourage and lead others. But my mind, heart, and body were all disconnected. The only way to become whole was to return to the pain—to reenter that darkness.

Jerry Sittser, a theologian and author who has suffered unimaginable loss, describes his own experience:

> The darkness comes, no matter how hard we try to hold it off. . . . I was frantically running west, trying desperately to catch the sun and remain in its fiery warmth and light. But I was losing the race. . . . I saw a vast darkness closing in on me. . . . [But later I realized] that the quickest way for anyone to reach the sun and the light of day is not to run west, chasing after the setting sun, but to head east, plunging into the darkness until [you] come to the sunrise.[56]

Whether or not loss is a defining experience for you, the wisdom remains: We can never reach the light without turning and heading directly into the darkness.

I did not expect my leadership development to require such

a demanding inner journey into my own loss and pain. But by pressing into what Soren Kierkegaard calls "an inward deepening" with God and my own soul, I have found a path to wholeness.[57]

In my experience, suffering either softens leaders or hardens them, but it never leaves them unchanged.

I have not reached a place of wholeness, and I'm certainly not a model of humility. But I'm on the way. My endlessly recurring temptation is to launch into the day, full of energy and strategy and hubris. But my weakness has become my most trusted advisor. True transformation—what I'm laboring for in the lives of men and women in my congregation and alongside me on our leadership team—requires a slower pace and a softer heart. Soul work is slow work.

When it comes to your own leadership journey and the pursuit of humility as a virtue, I simply echo Mother Teresa's words, "Choose always the more difficult task."[58]

May God bless you and keep you on the most difficult journey you'll ever make.

— *JEREMY LINNEMAN is lead pastor of Trinity Community Church in Columbia, Missouri.*

What About You?

"Search me, God, and know my heart; test me and know my anxious thoughts. See if there is any offensive way in me, and lead me in the way everlasting."

— Psalm 139:23–24 NIV

Reflect

» What temptations has success brought into your life?

» How would you practically define humility?

» Is listening to understand someone, asking for forgiveness, or being willing to be vulnerable difficult for you?

» What have you been holding onto that you would be willing to trust God for?

Record:

Write down your thoughts, feelings, action steps, questions, and anything else God reveals to your heart.

_____

_____

_____

_____

_____

_____

Remember

- Leaders realize that less of us and more of God is the winning combination for every circumstance in life.

- Leaders understand that success tends to promote an attitude of self-sufficiency and arrogance, which are opposed by God.

- Leaders view humility as a gift of grace forged over time in the context of his or her complete surrender to the will and the way of Someone much greater.

NOTES

1. Tasha Eurich, interviewed by Knowledge@Wharton, June 14, 2017, transcript.

2. Daniel Goleman, "What Makes a Leader," in *HBR's 10 Must Reads on Leadership* (Boston: Harvard Business School Publishing, 2011), 1–2.

3. Brennan Manning, *The Ragamuffin Gospel* (Colorado Springs: Multnomah Publishers, 1990, 2000), 26.

4. Timothy Keller, *Prayer* (Westminster, Md.: The Penguin Group, 2014), 30.

5. Richard Ben Cramer, *Joe DiMaggio: The Hero's Life* (New York: Simon and Schuster, 2000), 519.

6. David Benner, *The Gift of Being Yourself* (Westmont, Ill.: InterVarsity Press, 2004), 92.

7. M. Basil Pennington, *True Self / False Self: Unmasking the Spirit Within* (New York: Crossroads, 2000), 31.

8. Ruth Barton, *Strengthening the Soul of Your Leadership* (Westmont, Ill.: InterVarsity Press, 2008), 13, 26.

9. Augustine, qtd. in Peter Scazzero, *Emotionally Healthy Spirituality: It's Impossible to Be Spiritually Mature While Remaining Emotionally Immature* (Grand Rapids: Zondervan, 2017), n.p.

10. Aldous Huxley, *Jesting Pilate* (St. Paul, Minn.: Paragon House, 1926, 1991), 129.

11. Parker Palmer, "Leading from Within: Reflections on Spirituality and Leadership." Presentation at the annual celebration dinner of the Indiana Office of Campus Ministries, March 1990.

12. C. S. Lewis, quoted in Rick Warren, *The Purpose Driven Life* (Grand Rapids: Zondervan, 2002), 80.

13. Henri Nouwen, *The Way of the Heart* (New York: Ballentine Books, 1981), 17–18.

14. Celestine Chua, "How to Build an Edge: Develop Your Talent Stack" on *Personal Excellence.* https://personalexcellence.co/blog/talent-stack/.

15. William Wilberforce, "Journal, Sunday, October 28, 1787," quoted in Robert Isaac Wilberforce and Samuel Wilberforce, *The Life of William Wilberforce* (New York: Cambridge University Press), 1:149.

16. Oswald Chambers, *Oswald Chambers: The Best from All His Books*, ed. Harry Verploegh (Nashville: Thomas Nelson, 1987), 35.

17. Kaja Perina, "Who Cares About Character?" in *Psychology Today* (May 2015), https://www.psychologytoday.com/intl/articles/201504/who-cares-about-character?collection=1084610.

18. Richard Rohr, *Just This: Prompts and Practices for Contemplation* (Albuquerque: CAC Publishing, 2017), 82.

19. Augustine, qtd. in "Musings on Augustine's 'deepest wound,'" *vmntblog.com*, April 27, 2015. http://vmntblog.com/2015/04/musings-on-augustines-deepest-wound.html. Accessed July 17, 2018.

20. Michael J. Socolow, "Six Minutes in Berlin," *Slate.com*, July 23, 2012. http://www.slate.com/articles/sports/ fivering_circus/2012/07/_1936_olympics_rowing_the_ greatest_underdog_nazi_defeating_american_olympic_ victory_you_ve_never_heard_of_.html. Accessed July 6, 2018.

21. Ibid.

22. Ibid.

23. Ibid.

24. Daniel James Brown, *The Boys in the Boat* (London: Penguin Books, 2014), 353.

25. Keller, *Prayer*, 119.

26. Peter F. Drucker, *Managing for the Future* (Abingdon, UK: Routledge, 2011), 139.

27. Stephen R. Covey, *Primary Greatness* (New York: Simon and Schuster, 2015), 95.

28. George Barna, *The Power of Team* (Colorado Springs: WaterBrook Press, 2001), 7–9.

29. The Quotations Page, http://www.quotationspage.com/ quotes/H._L._Mencken/ (accessed June 26, 2018).

30. Peter F. Drucker, *Managing the Non-Profit Organization* (New York: HarperCollins Publishers, 1990), 19.

31. J. Oswald Sanders, *Spiritual Leadership,* revised edition (Chicago: Moody Press, 1967), 36.

32. Crawford W. Lorritts Jr., *Leadership as an Identity* (Chicago: Moody Publishers, 2009), 131.

33. James C. Collins, *Good to Great* (New York: HarperCollins Publishers, 2001), 21.

34. Bob Buford, *Drucker and Me* (Nashville: Worthy Publishing, 2014), 65.

35. Brother Lawrence and Frank Laubach, *Practicing His Presence* (n.p.: Christian Books, 1973), 59.

36. Brother Lawrence, *The Practice of the Presence of God, and The Spiritual Maxims* (Cosimo: New York, 2006), 68.

37. A. W. Tozer, *The Divine Conquest* (Harrisburg, PA: Christian Publishing, 1950), 26, 67.

38. Mother Teresa, *No Greater Love* (Novato, Calif.: New World Library, 2002), 85.

39. Timothy Keller, *The Prodigal God* (New York: Riverhead Books, 2008), 41–42.

40. Brother Lawrence, qtd. in Sheldon Cheney, *Men Who Have Walked with God* (Whitefish, Mont.: Kessinger Publishing, 1945), 303.

41. William R. Smith, *Quiet Time* (Little Rock, Ark.: Cross Reference Books, 1998), 27.

42. Charles Spurgeon, *The Treasury of David* (Peabody, Mass.: Hendrickson Publishers, 1876), via *The Spurgeon Archive*, Psalm 37.

43. David G. Benner, *Presence and Encounter* (Ada, Mich.: Brazos Press, 2014), 24.

44. Henri Nouwen, *Making All Things New: An Invitation to the Spiritual Life* (New York: HarperCollins Publishers, 1981), 69.

45. John Dickson, *Humilitas: A Lost Key to Life, Love, and Leadership* (Grand Rapids: Zondervan, 2011), 120.

46. David Brooks, *The Road to Character* (New York: Random House, 2015), xii.

47. Dickson, *Humilitas*, 70.

48. Mark Strom, *Arts of the Wise Leader* (Auckland, New Zealand: Sophos, 2007), 129.

49. Bob Dirgo, "What I Learned from Mother Teresa," *National Catholic Register*, Sept. 1, 2016. http://www.ncregister. com/daily-news/what-i-learned-from-mother-teresa.

50. Patti Armstrong, "Mother Teresa's 15 Tips to Help You Become More Humble," *National Catholic Register,* Nov. 21, 2016. http://www.ncregister.com/blog/armstrong/ mother-teresas-15-tips-to-help-you-become-more-humble.

51. Jim Collins, *Good to Great* (New York: Harper Collins Publishers, 2001), 35.

52. Ibid, 39.

53. Steven R. Covey, A. R. Merrill, and R. R. Merrill, *First Things First: To Live, to Love, to Learn, to Leave a Legacy* (New York: Free Press, 2003), 72–73.

54. "20 Leadership Quotes from Louie Giglio," 2014 Global Leadership Summit, Willow Creek Association, October 5, 2014.

55. Brooks, *The Road to Character*, xi.

56. Jerry L. Sittser, *A Grace Disguised: How the Soul Grows Through Loss* (Grand Rapids: Zondervan, 1995, 2004), 40–42.

57. *International Kierkegaard Commentary: Eighteen Upbuilding Discourses*, ed. Robert L. Perkins (Macon, Ga.: Mercer University Press, 2003), 56.

58. Armstrong, "Mother Teresa's 15 Tips to Help You Become More Humble."

BILL WELLONS

and his wife Carolyn helped found Fellowship Bible Church in Little Rock, Arkansas, in 1977. For thirty years he served that congregation as teaching pastor and chairman of the elder board. From its beginning, Fellowship has been involved in planting other churches. In 1999, Bill helped launch Fellowship Associates, a ministry started by Fellowship to foster church planting. In 2005, Bill moved full time to Fellowship Associates, serving as Executive Director of its Church Planting Residency Program. Fellowship Associates has been involved in planting one hundred churches, and those churches have planted an additional one hundred churches. Bill has also helped establish eight more residency programs to train pastors in the process of starting churches.

Bill and Carolyn have served as speakers with FamilyLife's nationwide Weekend to Remember events. Together, they co-authored *Getting Away to Get It Together*. Joining with Dr. Robert M. Lewis, Bill helped develop *The Great Adventure* DVD series for Men's Fraternity, and he and Lloyd Reed are co-authors of *Unlimited Partnership*.

Bill and Carolyn were married in 1970 and have three children and eleven grandchildren.

What Really Matters! is also available as an ebook at Amazon.com

CPSIA information can be obtained
at www.ICGtesting.com
Printed in the USA
BVHW07s2032221018
530920BV00001B/8/P